UNDIVIDED

A Greater Sense of Urgency in Reversing the Trend of Biblical Unbelief

Shawn Hyland

Publishing Services provided by: BelieversPress
Cover design: Dugan Design Group
Interior design and typeset: Michelle VanGeest

ISBN: Softcover 978-0-578-16762-6
ePUB 978-0-578-16763-3
MOBI 978-0-578-16764-0
Library of Congress Control Number: 2015913032

Printed in the United States of America

Table of Contents

Foreword 5
Preface — A Certain Sound 7
Introduction — Reverse the Trend of Biblical Unbelief 15

Section I — The UnBelief
Chapter 1 — It Has Begun 29
Chapter 2 — Absence of Accountability 45
Chapter 3 — Wrong Side of History 61

Section II — The Core Belief
Chapter 4 — God is the Creator and is sovereign over His creation 91
Chapter 5 — The Bible is 100% true and its moral teachings apply today 103
Chapter 6 — The devil is real, not merely a symbolic figure of evil 121
Chapter 7 — Man is sinful and saved by grace 133
Chapter 8 — Jesus is the sinless Savior, the Son of God 145

Section III — The UnDivided
Chapter 9 — Foundation to the Consummation 159
Chapter 10 — The Spirit of Lawlessness 181
Chapter 11 — The Urgency of the Hour 203

Final Word — Authentic Awakening 213
Notes 217
Author 227

Foreword

For generations, the adversary of our souls has been successful in dividing the church over non-essential doctrinal issues and peripheral matters that have been irrelevant to fulfilling our purpose. In the meantime, competing worldviews have captivated our culture's consciousness, relegating people of faith to barren backwaters far from the positions of influence that God always intended us to occupy. In his book *Undivided*, Shawn Hyland lays out the case for the body of Christ coming together around core beliefs to defend our faith and contend with the spirits of darkness to convert the souls of men.

Shawn was radically saved from a rebellious and destructive lifestyle. He is a graduate of Valor Christian College, where even as a student he displayed the characteristics that mark his ministry. He thinks deeply, sees clearly, argues persuasively and loves genuinely. He will challenge you, inform you and provoke you to become a culturally incorrect agent of redemptive change in your family and community.

Pastor Rod Parsley
World Harvest Church
Columbus, OH
Breakthrough Ministries

Preface

A Certain Sound

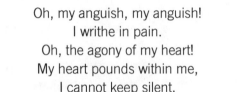

Oh, my anguish, my anguish!
I writhe in pain.
Oh, the agony of my heart!
My heart pounds within me,
I cannot keep silent.
For I have heard the sound of the trumpet;
I have heard the battle cry.
Jeremiah 4:19

But if the watchman sees the sword coming and does not blow
the trumpet to warn the people and the sword comes and takes
someone's life, that person's life will be taken because of their
sin, but I will hold the watchman accountable for their blood.
Ezekiel 33:6

Again, if the trumpet does not sound a clear call,
who will get ready for battle?
1 Corinthians 14:8

Joshua's campaigns for the conquest of the Promised Land yielded greater success than anyone in Israel dared hope. With the exception of a brief setback at the little town of Ai, God had undertaken to supernaturally assist the Israelites in dispossessing the Canaanites. From the time of the first victory at Jericho to the overthrow of the last enemy stronghold, Joshua's battles had been accompanied by the sound of the trumpet. After a generation of wilderness wandering, the ancient Israelites finally settled in their promised land. Their continued success would depend upon them fulfilling some promises on their part. Unfortunately, and at the expense of their grandchildren and their countless future progeny, they became entangled in the pagan cultures and practices of the cultures which surrounded them. A unique nation that was formed in the crucible of conflict through the mighty works of God's providential power over Pharaoh was slowly corrupted into the image of the false gods which enticed the pagan masses with empty souls. Israel experienced a demise that was as lamentable as it was preventable.

What God intended was reinvented. Their conquest was compromised. By refusing to carry out specific instructions to cleanse their land, they caused an endless cycle of regret that could only be rectified by repentance, which would lead to restoration.

This book is the long awaited, much anticipated "certain sound," comparable to the war trumpet of epic battles in the ages of antiquity. Now a new campaign is underway. God's people stand on the brink of a land filled with promises, but that is occupied by adversarial forces no less formidable than the pagan people who populated ancient Canaan. Without a certain sound announcing the beginning of an offensive action, who will prepare themselves for battle?

I intend to blow a trumpet that will summon the church to prepare to fight for the faith, awaken the virgin Bride and proclaim the return of Christ. Critics say it is impossible. Skeptics say it is unattainable. My Bible tells me it is inevitable—and it is already happening.

On January 25, 2014, at the steps of the New Jersey State House in the capital city of Trenton, I was privileged to witness the launch of the "We Stand — UNDIVIDED" campaign. Despite brutally cold and inclement weather, pastors and lay ministers alike stood at the halls of power, not to protest, but to proclaim the gospel and core Christian beliefs over New Jersey.

The trumpet was blown and the Church responded. Race, religion and relationships which divided us were now trumped by the timeless truths which had always united us. Pastors committed to monthly prayer gatherings strategically spread throughout the region as different local churches hosted times of intercession. Corporate worship nights were filled to near capacity as congregations gathered in one church with two other church worship teams leading the service. We submitted, God did it and that settles it—or I should say, that started it.

Nehemiah did not see Israel's glory days, but he heard stories of how it used to be. He returned to Jerusalem to find that God's people had the right to worship, yet lacked the safety and the pride of their once holy nation's capital. His call to action was simple, but powerful. He purposed to lead an effort to rebuild the walls of the city. He persuaded the elders, despite opposition by the mainstream culture, to grab a hammer and go to work. Ezra the scribe held a public rally in the town square for the reading of the Book of the Law to remind God's chosen people of who they were and what they believed. Eventually, this renewed emphasis on the word of God restored not only a nation, but a sense of sanctity and distinctiveness concerning Israel's relationship with God and their unique position in God's plan—even though they were considered cultural outsiders. Furthermore, this renewed faith caused a massive celebration which required every Levite from all the towns to gather in cooperation to serve side by side to accommodate the needs of the reinvigorated worshippers. Israel's spiritual comeback after the exile is the Biblical precedent for which I write and labor. The tribes coming together to rally around and be reminded of the Book of the Law, in our dispensation, the Gospel of Christ and the Christian Faith.

None of my generation has seen a revival that even approximates the Great Awakenings that shook America to its core many years ago. However, I have read enough and seen enough to know it is not like it used to be. I called the spiritual elders of the Jersey Shore to reverse the trend of biblical unbelief, similar to Nehemiah's efforts to rebuild. As in that day, our right to worship seems secure, but the Church finds herself weakened and vulnerable within our nation. We converged on our state capital, with an Ezra-like energy, for the proclamation of our beliefs, and to a greater extent, to proclaim our identity as Christians. Unity among the modern Levites was reestablished and a platform for the renewal of collective ministry was built.

The books of Ezra and Nehemiah both describe Israel coming together as one man to restore their nation. They declined the help offered by other inhabitants who falsely said that they would commit to serve and worship the same God. Israel's leaders wisely chose to avoid repeating what their forefathers had done by assimilating into the culture, which led to being consumed and conquered by the culture.

"We Stand—UNDIVIDED" is not a bland ecumenicalism of

blind unity to embrace and affirm doctrines that promote lifestyles of lasciviousness and humanistic heresies. What I recommend is not a broad circle of inclusiveness, but a definite plumb line of division. The immovable line of truth has been outlined on the vast ground of a globally connected world by none other than Jesus Christ, the Branch Himself.

> In those days and at that time
> I will make a righteous Branch sprout from David's line;
> he will do what is just and right in the land.
> **Jeremiah 33:15**

The reapers are prepared and awaiting final instructions. In accordance with Matthew 13, the sons of the Kingdom have been empowered with a greater spirit of boldness and balanced with a greater sense of God's burden than ever before.

Not only must we rekindle the fire that is incumbent upon every generation, but we need to respond with an urgency that surpasses all but a few generations before us. There are risks and rewards that will inevitably await us. Preaching the kingdom of God will automatically produce a variety of responses and reactions, including faith, but also fierce resistance. We must prepare ourselves for this. The moment a hint of persecution threatens to displace our self-centered bubble of Western individualism, we frantically attempt to restore its equilibrium, rather than rejoice for being counted worthy to suffer for Christ.

> The apostles left the Sanhedrin, rejoicing because they had
> been counted worthy of suffering disgrace for the Name.
> **Acts 5:41**

Instead, we hire branding experts who professionally polish our preaching, redefine our message and repackage our ministry to be more appealing and attractive to an unbelieving secular society. Offense? Scandals? Rejection? It might be too first century for most, but not for our Christian brothers scattered in house churches in Asia and bombed out churches in Arabia. Nor is rejection for the cross of Christ too great a price to pay for a remnant of sold-out saints, whose number I expect to be counted among in the last days—which are also these days.

The campaign, "We Stand — UNDIVIDED" is a prophetic message for a bold, strong and unified Church to regain the passion, the urgency and the authority to reverse the trend of Biblical unbelief in preparation for His second coming.

The Five Core Beliefs of the UNDIVIDED:

1. God is the Creator and is sovereign over His creation
2. The Bible is 100 percent true, and its moral teachings apply today
3. The devil is real and not merely a symbolic figure of evil
4. Man is sinful and saved by grace
5. Jesus is the sinless Savior, the Son of God

The book's chapters are divided into three sections. First, the Unbelief section will assess the downward trend of Biblical faith in our culture, and more broadly throughout Western civilization. Coincidence and chance are not the scapegoats. Old religious methods are not at fault. The clear and present danger of opposing and aggressive world views openly and blatantly hostile to the Christian faith have infiltrated our Judeo-Christian heritage and replaced it with humanism and atheism. The result is a great loss of faith hardened by an attitude of indifference. Nigel Barber in his book *Why Atheism will Replace Religion* predicts that by the year 2041, there will be more atheists than believers.[1]

> ...while evildoers and impostors will go from bad to worse, deceiving and being deceived. But as for you, continue in what you have learned and have become convinced of, because you know those from whom you learned it.
> **2 Timothy 3:13-14**

Second, the Core Belief section will consist of three divisions for each individual topic. The Revealed Knowledge part lists Bible verses that support the individual Core Belief topic. Then, the Reasons to Know section will educate and empower believers using apologetics and arguments as evidence to support our beliefs. Further, taking our spiritual beliefs and applying them to our physical, practical world, the Reality Known division will allow us to understand a cursed fallen world through the unchanging and clear lens of Scripture that each Core Belief represents.

Bible knowledge is near elementary levels within many of our local churches. Church services are skewed to *encourage* at the expense of *equipping*. Education is the primary ambition for the secularist. The Church in contrast shuts down Sunday Schools. Ordinary people of faith are unable to accurately communicate their faith or even answer simple surveys to describe their personal beliefs. Most Christians cannot discern the difference between a theistic belief in God and a deistic belief in "a god." George Barna, in his book *The Seven Faith Tribes* noted through years of research, "Most people are unconcerned about philosophical issues such as truth and worldview. They behave inconsistently doing one thing that smacks of a secular humanist orientation and following up with a behavior that reflects a Christian theist orientation and then another action that suggest a postmodern perspective."[2]

> Dear friends, although I was very eager to write to you about
> the salvation we share, I felt compelled to write and urge you to
> contend for the faith that was once for all entrusted
> to God's holy people.
> **Jude 3**

Finally, the Undivided section will reveal the timeline of the Church Age, the responsibility in proclaiming the Kingdom of God in preparation of the return of Christ, and consider the future of global persecution by progressive and domineering secular governments. Religious liberty is irrefutably being challenged in the courts through legislation and lawsuits at an alarming rate.

Through the dim and isolated view of America's Christian experience, most believers are passive to the possibility of losing our freedom of religion. Their indifference stems from a misunderstanding of the categoric difference between freedom of religion and freedom of worship.

The former is the right to freely express your religious views in the public sphere and marketplace without the fear of retribution. The latter is the right to privately assemble for ceremonial rituals — songs, sermons, and sacraments.

It seems most believers would rather practice a private faith un-challenged by the world. This is becoming less and less likely, and even impossible. Historically, universities were the beachhead of the onslaught against the Christian faith, but the lines have been redrawn. The extent and overreach of such virulent opposition to historic Christianity has now reared its head in the military branches, overtly affecting our active duty soldiers and heroes. Mikey Weinstein, founder of the Military Religious Freedom Foundation, has surprising access to top Pentagon and Air Force officials. He claims to be at war—but with whom? In a 2007 interview, Weinstein said, "I'm at war... We battle the Christian Taliban."[3]

"Now, Lord, consider their threats and enable your
servants to speak your word with great boldness.
Stretch out your hand to heal and perform signs and wonders
through the name of your holy servant Jesus."
After they prayed, the place where they were meeting
was shaken. And they were all filled with the Holy Spirit
and spoke the word of God boldly.
All the believers were one in heart and mind.
Acts 4:29-33

The trumpet has sounded—assemble the tribes, the congregations, the fellowships and even the denominations. The "certain sound" of our Core Beliefs is sounding a loud and distinct note. The strategy of isolating ourselves into the cultural corner by perfecting the Sunday morning worship experience, hoping "they" will come has not worked. "They" are bombarded daily with

> Through the dim and isolated view of America's Christian experience, most believers are passive to the possibility of losing our freedom of religion. Their indifference stems from a misunderstanding of the categoric difference between freedom of religion and freedom of worship.

tens of thousands of anti-Christian secular humanistic messages. When Demosthenes was asked what was to be done about the decline of Athens, his reply was, "I will give what I believe is the fairest and truest answer: Don't do what you are doing now."

I intend to cause an awareness of our situation—defined in the New Oxford Dictionary as "...having knowledge or perception of a situation or fact...concerned and well-informed about a particular situation or development." [4] I also expect to help accomplish an awakening, "...an act or moment of becoming suddenly aware of something...the beginning or rousing of something." [5] While I am concerned that the dreadful apostasy and the dryness of apathy, which are sure signs of spiritual decline, are not completely preventable or reversible, I cannot neglect my duty to my Sovereign and my generation.

Our world is far different today than it was forty years ago. In forty more years, it will be even more drastically different than we find it today. History proves and prophecy predicts that the moral, spiritual, political and financial norms of our world will progressively become worse. Lawlessness is running rampant, many have left the faith and a great delusion has led our culture astray. The final hour, which I believe will also be the finest hour of the Church, has come!

Introduction

Reverse the Trend of
Biblical Unbelief

When Jesus landed and saw a large crowd, he had compassion
on them, because they were like sheep without a shepherd.
So he began teaching them many things.
Mark 6:34

"The reason I was born and came into the world is to testify to
the truth. Everyone on the side of truth listens to me."
John 18:37

It is written: "I believed; therefore I have spoken."
Since we have that same spirit of faith,
we also believe and therefore speak…
2 Corinthians 4:13

"Then it is Athanasius against the world!" said the young cleric, not yet 30 years old, during the First Council of Nicaea. *Athanasius contra mundum*; the legacy of persistence to truth. While scholars fragmented with illusions of new sophisticated theologies during the summer of 325 AD, Athanasius remained decisive. Despite being banished and brutally outcast, Athanasius fought diligently against overwhelming odds to triumphantly persuade hundreds of bishops to interpret the Bible and the divinity and humanity of Christ in an orthodox manner. The basics of faith, taken for granted today, were nearly lost early in the Constantine era seventeen centuries ago. One man graciously took the lead and received in return the tongue lashings. Defined by some as controversial and divisive, Athanasius held firm as he resisted fierce pressure from priests, bishops,

15

the Pope, the emperor and his closest aids; even the whole world was against him. His choice: take the narrow road, be a pioneer, turn the world upside down. The result: the misguided bishops caved with Holy Ghost conviction. The true Universal Church was united without compromise or doctrinal error. The truth won. It always does — when it fights back.

Confrontation at appropriate times and with appropriate methods is Christlike. Misused with wrong motivations, it can also be viewed as condemning and critical. Jesus was confrontational. John MacArthur, in his book *The Jesus You Can't Ignore*, vividly, made the modern Christian reader aware of a Jesus who boldly stood for truth. Controversy and confrontation were social media hashtags which emphasized his teaching encounters with the self-righteous elites that paraded around society. MacArthur states, "The Great Shepherd Himself was never far from open controversy with the most conspicuously religious inhabitants in all of Israel. Almost every chapter of the Gospels makes some reference to His running battle with the chief hypocrites of His day, and He made no effort whatsoever to be winsome in His encounters with them."[1]

At a base level, we misattribute Jesus' impatience with hypocrisy and self-righteousness, as if the Messiah was against the religion of the Pharisees. Jesus perfected religion. In his culture, the most dedicated and devout had a love for The Law of Moses and strived to honor and uphold it. Jesus exclusively fulfilled The Law of Moses. In retrospect, he was the most 'religious' man who ever lived.

> "Do not think that I have come to abolish the Law or the Prophets; I have not come to abolish them but to fulfill them. For truly I tell you, until heaven and earth disappear, not the smallest letter, not the least stroke of a pen, will by any means disappear from the Law until everything is accomplished. Therefore anyone who sets aside one of the least of these commands and teaches others accordingly will be called least in the kingdom of heaven, but whoever practices and teaches these commands will be called great in the kingdom of heaven. For I tell you that unless your righteousness surpasses that of the Pharisees and the teachers of the law, you will certainly not enter the kingdom of heaven."
> **Matthew 5:17-20**

The incarnation of divine, unconditional love, Christ the Messiah, was not against the law. He, in essence, increased the difficulty of the law by adding our thoughts and desires as equal sins with our actions. The Sermon on the Mount was the prime example of Jesus teaching us how far we were as fallen humanity, collectively and individually, from pleasing the will of God found in the Law. The moral high ground was leveled. Truth brought hope for the sinner and humility for the self-righteous. The Pharisees were furious. Elites frown at equality.

God opposes the proud, but gives grace to the humble.
James 4:6

The underlining core belief of the Pharisees was the insistence of not needing a savior (Nicodemus being the statistical anomaly of the strong headed Pharisaical attitude). Such a high regard for oneself is breathtaking. They believed their intellect on matters concerning The Law of Moses was sufficient. It was a wedge so stubborn that Jesus did not attempt to remove it. Scripture never records a moment where Jesus said to the self-righteous, "Come, follow me." Their stiff necks would not easily follow and would prove nearly impossible to move. Finally, they could bear the Nazarite no more. Their plan was flawless and to this day still in operation. Silence the truth by arresting the Christ and massively misinform 'the folks' to convince them such truth is hateful or in Christ's day, heretical. Save yourself, not us, they flippantly mocked.

The people stood watching, and the rulers even sneered at him.
They said, "He saved others; let him save himself if he is
God's Messiah, the Chosen One."
Luke 23:35

The hardness of such intellectual pride found its soft spot when the risen Jesus confronted Saul, the Pharisee in Acts 9. The outcome was all together different than His other encounters with Pharisees before the resurrection. Jesus loved Saul as He did Caiaphas, the high priest that had him arrested and crucified. The challenge that Jesus faced was how to humble a stiff necked, no need to be saved, intellectual, aggressive hater towards all things Christian (soon after to be known as Christian). In physical stature, Saul was a man. In his unregenerate soul, Saul was an ox.

> "Saul, Saul, why are you persecuting Me?...
> It is hard for you to kick against the goads."
> **Acts 9:4-5**

The term 'kicking against the goads' was a Greek proverb used in agriculture. The term described how a stiff-necked ox would kick back against the spear a farmer used to prod the animal in the right direction while plowing. Oxen were inherently too stubborn and too strong. Jesus had masterfully developed a new approach to deal with an intellectual ox. Prick him. He will kick back but the love of God never quits and never fails.

Christ won. Athanasius won. The theory is well proven. Truth wins, whether in opposition to an ox or in proposition of the orthodox. It must fight. It must prick. It must relentlessly persevere.

Western Civilization finds itself today entangled in the debate of objective, moral truth versus relative, subjective, personal beliefs. Modern Pharisees and Sadducees are emboldened with educational credentials of unbelief and biblical higher criticism. Not surprisingly, the most respected and historical university in the Western world is also one of the most hostile and ox-like to Christian beliefs: Oxford University, in the city of Oxford, England. Yes, the pun is intended.

Honorably, Oxford University is the home of C.S. Lewis and Ravi Zacharias, two of the most influential Christian apologists of our time. Conversely, it also boasts of Richard Dawkins an aggressive atheist, and the famed theoretical physicist Stephen Hawking, an admitted atheist. Undeniably, the average student is indoctrinated by atheist professors and faculty to disregard the claims of Christ and Christianity. The underlining core belief of the new "Ox"ford atheist is eerily similar to the ancestral ox of the first century Pharisee. Namely, the insistence that one does not need a savior. The Humanist Manifesto II, written in 1973 says, "No deity will save us; we must save ourselves." This familiar rhetoric was used by those who spitefully chose a similar humanistic philosophy at the time of Christ.

Hence the spirit of our age. Man is purely physical. There is no God. The Bible is untrue for it speaks of God. There is no devil for there is no God or spirit realm. Man is a byproduct of genetics and the environment. There is no sin. There is no savior. We save ourselves.

The chains of morality and judgment have been unfettered. The enemy is not religion, overall, but strictly Christ and the Christian faith. The glorious promise of a morally unrestrained, new global world is the utopian goal of the humanist, atheist, statist and secularist.

The intellectual pursuit is lofty but the casualties are reckless nihilism by some and for the less disciplined, gross hedonism.

Pastors and denominational leaders deem church attendance as the measuring stick of ministry success. The most zealous faithful, known as Captive Christians, in George Barna's *The Seven Faith Tribes*, go to church once per week. The average worship service is 90 minutes or slightly less than 1% of a person's week. Less than 1% is the amount of time the most sold-out among us spend in church. As a result, less than 1% is the amount of young adults who have a biblical worldview.

The time exposed to secular reasoning, void of the knowledge of God, far exceeds the time spent in church by a minority of 'Christians,' a term I must loosely use for the sake of national surveys. Christians, whether evangelical, traditional or liberal have a split screen view of the world and of their perceived faith. The non-religious, secular screen is in high definition. The 'Christ is the only way' evangelicalism screen is the fuzzy, antenna-fed, comical and yesteryear screen; routinely labeled and set aside on the fringe of the mainstream, pluralistic society.

> The chains of morality and judgment have been unfettered. The enemy is not religion, overall, but strictly Christ and the Christian faith. The glorious promise of a morally unrestrained, new global world is the utopian goal of the humanist, atheist, statist and secularist.

Athanasius was against the world for the truth. Jesus came into the world to testify of the truth. Jesus described the Holy Spirit as the Spirit of Truth (John 14:17, 15:26, 16:13). Jesus claimed to be the truth (John 14:6). I will stand for the truth. Will you?

> "The reason I was born and came into the world is to testify to the truth. Everyone on the side of truth listens to me."
> **John 18:37**

Humanists, atheists and others have intermingled their views to develop points of belief and conflict, which over the process of five decades, have pushed the tipping point of popular opinion against the church and rejected biblical truth by embracing non-religious thought as the only valid and reasonable path for America. These leaders and think tanks have mastered the realms of marketing, message development and organizational branding to successfully make converts of Bible believers in one generation, into bible unbelievers in the next. Atheists did not practice door to door evangelism with a hopeless message of a universe and existence without God. The humanists did not plan and promote community family days to share a temporal and pleasurable view of man to their neighbors. Unlike the success stories of Jesus and Athanasius, we are losing Christian truth in the marketplace of ideas. Why? We do not prick and we do not fight. The Church strives for popularity at the expense of silencing her prophets.

Truth has the uncanny ability to change people and the ability to offend people. The Church has failed in passing on and communicating the authentic faith to our culture and to our congregations. How can this be? We endeavor ministry events with excellence, we feed the poor, we rebuild homes, we construct computerized check-in children's ministries, we turn down the overhead lights and aromatize our lobbies with freshly brewed coffee. We pride and market our compassionate accomplishments which we have done 'in the name of the Lord' for the community (without literally mentioning his name) and what we can do for the prospective seeker's family of all ages. Conversely, in all this striving and labor, we have mistakenly sacrificed the truth. Focused more heavily on gaining the acceptance and approval of our community, we forsook the reason God sent us into our community, to proclaim and herald the truth.

Jesus, our perfect example, and the Apostle Paul, our more practical example, distinctly and with a unified tone, communicate to us the core sent mission and responsibility of ministry. Preach!

"Let us go somewhere else—
to the nearby villages—
so I can preach there also.
That is why I have come." — *Jesus*
Mark 1:38

"I must proclaim the good news of the kingdom of God to the
other towns also, because that is why I was sent." — Jesus
Luke 4:43

For Christ did not send me to baptize, but to preach the
gospel—not with wisdom and eloquence, lest the cross of Christ
be emptied of its power. For the message of the cross is
foolishness to those who are perishing, but to us who are being
saved it is the power of God. — Paul
1 Corinthians 1:17-18

Preaching the gospel, the Kingdom of God and the cross of Christ
was the reason for being sent. The Church has been known for political
work in our support of moral causes. I respectively encourage us to
continue sharing our faith and guiding principles with our representatives. The Church has been known, more recently, for our active work
in addressing social injustices ranging from global poverty, human
trafficking to immigration reform. I urge us to carry on such worthy
causes of compassion to rightfully demonstrate the fullness of God's
love for man in every culture and class. However, neither of these are
the primary reasons the Church exists on earth. Jesus healed as part
of His mission. Paul baptized as part of his mission. We sign petitions
to elected officials and distribute much needed items to those in need
as part of our mission. Still, preaching truth is the fundamental and
foremost function of the Church. Why? As the Pentecostal amen corner
abruptly chimes in, "the devil is a liar!"

Jesus came to them and said, "All authority in heaven and on
earth has been given to me. Therefore go and make disciples
of all nations, baptizing them in the name of the Father and
of the Son and of the Holy Spirit, and teaching them to obey
everything I have commanded you. And surely I am with you
always, to the very end of the age."
Matthew 28:18-20

Preaching causes conflicts. It's powerful, persuasive and the
overall purpose is to cause reflection and repentance. Rod Parsley, a
general of the faith, specifically in the art of homiletics, describes the

preaching of the cross in New Testament terms, "The cross is offensive. Its implications, an outrage. Its message, scandalous. These are not the assertions of a postmodern skeptic or a humanistic university professor. This is the plain declaration of the Bible."[2] In Parsley's book, The Cross, he digs deeper into the reasons why preaching truth is unpopular and unacceptable. These include an affront to man's pride, man's wisdom and man's self righteousness.

The gospel strikes at the soul and spirit of man as it pierces and consumes the heart of the hearers. It increases faith and decreases pride. No surprise, the word of God is a double-edged sword (Hebrews 4:12). The word is synonymous with Christ (John 1:1), who is God (Section III, Core Belief). God is a consuming fire (Hebrews 12:29, Deuteronomy 9:3). The word of God is accurately illustrated as a flaming sword. Such a mighty weapon was used by God in the Garden of Eden to protect man from accessing the tree of life. Man is ingrained with fallen DNA. He detests the truth because he desires to be the god of this world, knowing good and evil for himself. His fallen nature shuns the truth as a moral boundary to enjoying paradise.

Today, much of the church is focused on the more crowd-pleasing features of our faith. We compromise the predominant role of preaching for the more comforting role of community service. We hold more in common with the United Way than the early, first century Hebrew sect known as The Way.

Biblical belief is at an all time low and our response is timid.

Many lack the courage to step out of our secularly prescribed and dictated corner of Sunday morning worship. The Christian faith is declining throughout Western Civilization, while the globe on a massive scale is having unprecedented revival. It's our watch. It's our failure.

Another famous soul winning preacher, Charles Finney, summed up this message, "The Decay of Conscience," in New York, Dec. 4, 1873, to America's clergy: "Brethren, our preaching will bear its legitimate fruits. If immorality prevails in the land, the fault is ours in a great degree. If there is a decay of conscience, the pulpit is responsible for it. If the public press lacks moral discrimination, the pulpit is responsible for it. If the church is degenerate and worldly, the pulpit is responsible for it. If the world loses its interest in religion, the pulpit is responsible for it. If Satan rules in our halls of legislation, the pulpit is responsible for it. If our politics become so corrupt that the very foundations of our government are ready to fall away, the pulpit is responsible for it. Let us not ignore this fact, my dear brethren; but let us lay it to heart, and be thoroughly awake to our responsibility in respect to the morals of this nation."[3]

The American church explodes when preaching encourages the congregations but leadership often writhes in discomfort when approached about a biblical view of marriage. The fear of man carries more weight than the fear of the Lord. Our preaching inevitably

> Biblical belief is at an all time low and our response is timid.

becomes powerless and loses the double-edged, flaming sword status. Our conscience is clear because our preaching is muddled. Precisely the way fallen man, 'being as god,' in the Garden would want it to be.

To reverse the trend of biblical unbelief we need a bold presentation of truth. We need an unrestrained boldness empowering the Church to proclaim Christ crucified, resurrected and soon returning to judge the living and the dead. We need more passion, urgency and authority. Forgive my repetitiveness: Boldness!

There is one word that uniquely is attributed to God and Him alone, "Holy." There is one word that authentically hallmarks the first century church, "Boldly."

But Barnabas took him, and brought him to the apostles,
and declared unto them how he had seen the Lord in the way,
and that he had spoken to him, and how he had preached
boldly at Damascus in the name of Jesus.
Acts 9:27

And he spake boldly in the name of the Lord Jesus, and
disputed against the Grecians: but they went about to slay him.
Acts 9:29

Long time therefore abode they speaking boldly in the Lord,
which gave testimony unto the word of his grace, and granted
signs and wonders to be done by their hands.
Acts 14:3

And he began to speak boldly in the synagogue: whom when
Aquila and Priscilla had heard, they took him unto them, and
expounded unto him the way of God more perfectly.
Acts 18:26

And he went into the synagogue, and spake boldly for the
space of three months, disputing and persuading the things
concerning the kingdom of God.
Acts 19:8

And for me, that utterance may be given unto me, that I may
open my mouth boldly, to make known the mystery of the
gospel, for which I am an ambassador in bonds: that therein I
may speak boldly, as I ought to speak.
Ephesians 6:19-20

In this hour of unbelief and lawlessness, we desperately need a full throttle gospel reaction. Jesus had the unpleasant experience of not knowing what to expect from town to town. His overall message never changed but the people did. He was stoned by some and worshipped by others but He, undeniably, always caused a reaction. Some repented and some retaliated but all responded. The Apostles were celebrated as gods by some and incarcerated as criminals by others but they always caused a reaction. The reaction is diverse and divisive, humility before God by some, hatred towards the messenger by others; a reaction nonetheless.

The call sounds provocative. I humbly submit it's more prophetic. This hour was prophesied to come. It is the hour when many would leave the faith and hate the truth. It is the hour when teachers surrender their integrity and give the people what they want to hear.

This is not the panic alarm of negativity. The sky is not falling but opening. Our Savior is returning.

He is not coming for a local church. He is coming for a body; for His bride. From charismatics to those holding views of cessationism, Christ is coming for us all. Revengeful and aggressive, the anti-christ spirit in this world is coming after us all. The Church has fought doctrinal disagreements with spirited debate for centuries. The Church became healthy when purged from heresies.

Times have now changed. The humanist and atheist have a goal of denying the existence of God, the divinity of Christ, the reliability and inerrancy of the Bible, the existence of the devil and man's fallen sinful nature in need of grace. Their desire to bring about a one world community without God should motivate our generation to teach our dogmatic

> This is not the panic alarm of negativity. The sky is not falling but opening. Our Savior is returning.

differences, such as Calvinism to Arminianism in our denominational times of worship but unite in the public square for the holy common faith. Regretfully, we criticize our Christian brethren at conferences and mock one another in blogs over the minors of our faith. Meanwhile, the anti-christian spirit which is emboldened in this present climate, with a fervency to attack the majors of our faith, goes unnoticed or unchallenged.

Nationally, we must recognize the aggressive assault against the Christian faith from atheists, educators and entertainers. In addition, we must acknowledge the threat to religious liberty which is regularly being challenged in the courts. The famous words of Pastor Martin Niemöller speaks volumes to us today for our inaction and indifference.

"First they came for the Socialists, and I did not speak out — Because I was not a Socialist. Then they came for the Trade Unionists, and I did not speak out — Because I was not a Trade Unionist. Then they came for the Jews, and I did not speak out — Because I was not a Jew. Then they came for me — and there was no one left to speak for me."

Celebrity Christianity is no more. The Acts of the Apostles which turned the world upside down (Acts 17:6) was balanced by persecution from the powerful. The cross of Christ is a positional place of self sacrifice and worldly rejection. Arenas and bookshelves are filled with messages and manuals to improve and enjoy this life, the life that Christ told us to lose. Humanism has infected the church. Our offensive counter to the sexual revolution which exalted man's pleasure was a new gospel of purpose; the spiritual laws in 60 seconds for God's plan to give us an abundant life. It is an intriguing strategy but not the one implemented by Christ. His ways are not our ways. We have in mind the things of men and not the things of God.

From that time Jesus began to show to His disciples that He must go to Jerusalem, and suffer many things from the elders and chief priests and scribes, and be killed, and be raised the third day. Then Peter took Him aside and began to rebuke Him, saying, "Far be it from You, Lord; this shall not happen to You!" But He turned and said to Peter, "Get behind Me, Satan! You are an offense to Me, for you are not mindful of the things of God, but the things of men." Then Jesus said to His disciples, "If anyone desires to come after Me, let him deny himself, and take up his cross, and follow Me."

Matthew 16:21-24

An awe of holiness, an attitude of humility and a hunger for the preaching of bold truth is coming on those for whom Christ is coming. The Church must leave the safe haven of convenience and comfort to engage the deception prevalent in our age. We must stand UNDIVIDED for the major fundamentals of the faith. This is the flaming sword used with divine skill through the preaching of the gospel. Such preaching will enact the hands of persecution against us.

Immediately following the call to the cross in Matthew 16, Jesus was transfigured in preparation for the physical trial He would eventually face. He received encouragement by seeing those who had gone before Him and hearing the voice of His well-pleased Father. He was surrounded by Moses, the pastoral, spiritual leader of God's people and Elijah, the bold, thundering prophetic voice. Two distinct gifts and anointings. Christ needed both and so do we. Pulpits are filled with godly Moses-like pastors. Where are the trumpets in the Spirit of Elijah? Where are those who choose to stand alone, outside the mainstream, who are despised by the secular and the religious? Where are those preparing the way of the Lord? Let us partner together to prepare the body of Christ for the days and years which are before us. Don't keep your distance. If they come for me and you do not speak out, be not overconfident, they will come for you, too. Together, "We Stand UNDIVIDED." Let them come for us, at least we are expecting them. Christ is also coming for us at an hour when we think not!

Section 1

The UnBelief

Chapter One

It Has Begun

The Spirit clearly says that in later times some will abandon the
faith and follow deceiving spirits and things taught by demons.
1 Timothy 4:1

At that time many will turn away from the faith and will betray
and hate each other, and many false prophets will appear
and deceive many people.
Matthew 24:10-11

For the time will come when people will not put up with
sound doctrine. Instead, to suit their own desires,
they will gather around them a great number of teachers to say
what their itching ears want to hear. They will turn their ears
away from the truth and turn aside to myths.
2 Timothy 4:3-4

Taps. Tomb of the Unknown Solider. Bagpipes. Amazing Grace. Chopin's Funeral March. A pallbearer reluctantly grows accustomed to such grief. The ceremony and tears are absorbed through an acquired professional mechanism to cope with the greatest enemy known to man. Insult me for my insensitive somber setting, but in a fallen world, decay and decomposition is unavoidable. The Church must come to terms with the obvious fact that the Christian faith is in decline throughout America, especially among the millennial generation.

Pastors and their leadership staff travel hundreds of miles to dozens of top notch church growth conferences, organized by successful ministries, with hopes of incorporating 'best practices' to increase the attendance and participation within their local church. America is an ideal culture for church growth with its capitalistic and competitive nature. Churches with the termed 'growth mentality' actively pursue the latest ideas to get a step ahead of the new church plant down the street. Church metrics are vital to track the growth and set organizational goals. Volunteers? Donor records? Sunday attendance? Visitor assimilation? Small groups? Year to date? Churches today use comparative studies from previous years to forecast the next three years. All this to attain that long awaited, new building project. Money...Metrics...Ministry.

Pastors gracefully blessed with large megachurches become heroes of the faith; admired and highly sought after speakers. At a superficial glance, attendance and giving records are the predominant measure of success. At a much deeper level, biblical faith and knowledge among the congregants is nearly off the radar of most churches.

A funeral offers an exceptional situation for a 'come to Jesus' moment. Most ministers throw out the bait and fish for men somewhere following Psalm 23 and John 11. Facing the death of a loved one is a personal time of reckoning. The Church of Western Civilization needs our own 'come to Jesus' day of reckoning.

We are either the Pallbearer or Paul-bearer Generation. We will either carry the Bible to its secular, socialist, humanist, atheist grave in the post-Christian 21st century as pallbearers carry the casket to its final resting place, or we will bear the burden of Paul the Apostle (Paul-bearer) and through his suffering, rejection, and boldness, turn our world upside down. Either way, the status quo does not remain.

Gas up the hearse and slide on the white gloves as pallbearers because, according to a 2009 Barna Research Survey, less than 1% of young adults, ages 18-23, had a biblical worldview. For the purposes of the survey, a "biblical worldview" was defined as believing that absolute moral truth exists; the Bible is totally accurate in all of the principles it teaches; Satan is considered to be a real being or force, not merely symbolic; a person cannot earn their way into Heaven by trying to be good or do good works; Jesus Christ lived a sinless life on earth; and God is the all-knowing, all-powerful creator of the world who still rules the universe today. In the research, anyone who held all of those beliefs was said to have a biblical worldview.[1]

Shockingly, the 5 Core Beliefs of *UnDivided*, so indispensable to the Christian faith, have been rejected as an insufficient belief system by an entire generation. The survey also concluded that only 9% of all American adults agree to these 5 Core Beliefs or biblical worldview. Who is to blame for such a staggering downward trend of biblical belief in our country? Liberal Universities? Possibly. Mainstream media? Probably. The Church of Jesus Christ? Absolutely! The number of self-proclaimed 'born again' Christians who confess to believe all 5 Core Beliefs is pitifully at 19%.

Stunningly, these statistics do not surprise the experts. George Barna, from the Barna Research group, who conducted the survey said, "Did you know that the moral values of people are generally decided by the time they reached the age of nine? Did you know that our foundational spiritual beliefs and commitments are typically ingrained by the age of 13? Were you aware that relational habits and patterns are pretty much molded by the age of 13? The lesson was clear, how we raise children before they reach high school age determines who they become for life."[2] In other words, before the liberal bias of slanted information common in universities and the news media ever reaches the gates of our children's souls, we have either failed or succeeded in passing on the faith.

> I am reminded of your sincere faith, which first lived in your grandmother Lois and in your mother Eunice and, I am persuaded, now lives in you also.
> **2 Timothy 1:5**

> Teach them (the law) to your children, talking about them when you sit at home and when you walk along the road, when you lie down and when you get up.
> **Deuteronomy 11:19**

Karl Marx famously said, "We must destroy the family...we must replace home education with social." Again, "Take away the heritage of the people, and they are easily persuaded." Public education is a major obstacle in teaching and imparting the faith to the next generation. At its core, it was established as a progressive institution to form a new socialist society without God or Biblical values as the foundation. Horace Mann, known as the Father of the American Public School System, rejected the Scriptures and the Trinity, and revealed the spirit behind secular social public education, "parents have given their children to our cause." [3]

John Dewey is the Father of Modern Education and the founder of the National Education Association. His infamous quote, "The great task of the school is to counteract and transform those domestic and neighborhood tendencies...the influence of home and church."

His beliefs, "There is no god. There is no soul. Hence, there are no needs for the props of traditional religion."

Distinctly, different voices had opposed such opinions about education at the founding of America. Noah Webster, the Father of American Scholarship and Education said in 1828, "In my view, the Christian religion is the most important and one of the first things in which all children, under a free government ought to be instructed. Additionally, founding father Benjamin Rush, Father of American Psychiatry, who started five schools and universities, agrees, "We profess to be republicans [not political party] and yet we neglect the only means of establishing and perpetrating our republican form of government; that is, the universal education of our youth in the principles of Christianity by the means of the Bible." With even greater foreknowledge he precisely predicted our modern incarceration and violence epidemic. "In contemplating the political institutions of the United States [if we remove the Bible from schools] I lament that we waste so much time and money punishing crimes and take so little pains to prevent them."

Ancient Israel forgot the Lord their God quickly after their supernatural and prosperous beginning. America has followed suit.

The Israelites did evil in the eyes of the Lord; they forgot the
Lord their God and served the Baals and the Asherahs.
Judges 3:7

They forgot the God who saved them,
who had done great things in Egypt,...
Psalm 106:21

A cry is heard on the barren heights, the weeping and pleading
of the people of Israel, because they have perverted their ways
and have forgotten the Lord their God.
Jeremiah 3:21

Each succeeding generation since World War II has progressively left the Christian faith at nearly the same rate. 60% of adults from the post-World War II generation have a biblical worldview. This number quickly dropped to 30% of adults who were coming of age during the sexual revolution and Woodstock generation. Another swift dip occurs immediately in Generation X, where just

> John Dewey is the Father of Modern Education and the founder of the National Education Association. His infamous quote, "The great task of the school is to counteract and transform those domestic and neighborhood tendencies...the influence of home and church."

over 4% of adults have a biblical worldview. Finally or fatally, however you choose to interpret the numbers, we are at last down to 1% for the Millennium Generation. Is the Pallbearer Generation becoming more believable? Does the secular grave await our precious faith?

According to a recent Gallup survey, 77% of Americans believe religion is losing its influence in the country. That's the highest percentage in more than 40 years.[4] In 2011, the Southern Baptist Convention, the largest denomination in the United States, announced the results of a survey showing a significant decline in baptisms and church membership. Ed Stetzer, a researcher with Lifeway Research, commented at that time, "This is not a blip. This is a trend. And the trend is one of decline."[5] In 2014, the SBC reported a 13% decrease in year to year water baptisms, the worst drop in 62 years.[6] More recently, the Pew Research Center released a study on the state of religion in the United States entitled "'Nones' on the Rise." The study brings into focus the increasing growth rate of those who do not identify with any religion at all. Nearly one-fifth of the US adult population and one-third of those under the age of 30 identify in this way; an increase from 15 percent just 5 years earlier.[7] In 2011, across the Atlantic, a report on the Church of England highlighted the challenges it was facing: aging congregations, faltering clergy recruitment and waning attendance.

While church leaders used words like "crisis" and "time bomb," the report predicted the church would likely be extinct within 20 years.[8] Czech president, Vaclav Havel, has rightly described Europe as "the first atheistic civilization in the history of mankind." [9] America has been following Europe's lead in music, fashion, democratic socialism and progressive values. We are not far behind in their unbelief and disdain for traditional Christianity.

The rehearsal of facts should cause a divine disturbance. America, and Western Civilization overall, is losing its faith and bluntly rejecting the truth of Scripture with more confidence and less conviction than ever before. It is one of the many well-defined tragedies of our age.

Our response is indefensible. The professing Church has become weak and weary in standing for the truth because we have become ignorant and uninspired by it. Content with getting our heads into heaven, we dismiss getting heaven into our heads as tedious and tiresome. People only stand for what they believe in. Hence, we refuse to hold our ground. We do not stand, because according to statistics, we do not believe! Less than 1 out of every 5 "born again" Christians have a biblical worldview.

It is written: "I believed; therefore I have spoken."
Since we have that same spirit of faith,
we also believe and therefore speak,...
2 Corinthians 4:13

The secular arena has sensed our weakness and our intimidation to stand. A hatred for the truth, embedded in the heart of man, is now amplified and socially acceptable. The trendsetters of culture have progressively and intensively slandered the Bible for their own agenda and purpose. Spanning from articulated atheists to outspoken, moral liberals fundamentally remaking the image of man, the Christian worldview has become the scapegoat for all things negative, whether politically, financially, morally or spiritually.

Our reply is flimsy, weak and shaky, while in contrast our God is powerful, sovereign and soon returning. The Church must find its voice and willpower to stand and speak or forever hold its peace and prophetic voice.

None of the statistics should catch us off guard. First, if we were watching and praying as instructed, we would have foreseen this dubious trend. Second, the Apostles warned us that a falling away from the faith, lawlessness, and deception would be evident in the last days. Jesus warned us that widespread deception would be common before His second coming.

> They perish because they refused to love
> the truth and so be saved.
> **2 Thessalonians 2:10**

> Watch out that no one deceives you.
> **Matthew 24:4**

The lack of truth coming from the Church, coupled with the abundance of misinformation from non-biblical institutions, makes deception more possible than in previous generations. The local clergy in years past had influence in their community. That influence has now been exchanged for mistrust. The Associated Press reveals that researchers at Gallup found 53% of Americans have lost trust in the clergy — the worst ratings in 40 years.[10]

Influence is defined in the New Oxford American Dictionary as "the capacity to have an effect on the character, development, or behavior of someone or something."[11] It does not take professional pollsters to conclude what is already apparent. Upon taking a brief look at the 'character and behavior' of adults, especially young adults in the Millennium Generation, it becomes clear the Church has not influenced them with biblical truth. George Barna gives us a structured pyramid of cultural influence, "The top tier of influence entities includes: family, public policy, and five-forms of media — movies, television, music, the Internet and books. We discovered an estimated 60% to 70% of a typical person's worldview and resulting behavior have been significantly shaped by the information and experience received from those seven sources. The middle tier of influence consists of about a dozen different entities such as schools, peers, athletes, and several more media forms — radio, video games, newspapers, and magazines. These influence 20% to 30% of a typical person's life decisions. The lowest tier, which usually has about 10% of the influence on a person's choices consisted of nearly 2 dozen entities including churches. ... In essence the data showed that we are typically impacted primarily by three major sources of input — family, media, and government." [12] The Church has been relegated to the bottom tier of influence. We could only hope that Jesus' Kingdom teaching, "the last will be first and the first last" would work in our favor this time!

Ordinarily, truth, worldview and apologetics are not major themes of discipleship goals within evangelical or mainline congregations. Rightfully so, most people do not seek after truth, knowledge or wisdom. A Miley Cyrus twerk will trend #1 on search engines, while simultaneously, Syrian President Assad's chemical attack has little interest to the online world.

Habitually, hype and humanism is the centerpiece of the Sunday morning sermon. The secular world has crafted us a small corner of influence. At arms length, they passively allow us to worship in our safe sanctuaries for 90 minutes of unchallenged influence to speak to a single digit fraction of the population in our surrounding community. Is the Church making good use of this opportunity to counteract the deception of the secularization which our congregants experience at their schools and occupations?

Faith and religion, we are informed by the secularists, are matters of the heart which are only appropriate and acceptable as a personal subjective truth kept reverently behind the walls of the church or the doors of your home. On the other hand, facts and science are matters of the head which dominate the public arena and dictate professionalism in every sphere of society. This undoubtedly has shaped the dualistic belief systems that are juggled by well-intentioned believers.

Our fascination with church metrics refocuses our efforts to emphasize less on equipping the saints with truth and instead, encourage the attendees with life-coaching idealism.

The Church on Sunday fails to prepare the saint for the work of the ministry. The vocational Christian falls prey to false messaging and is unable to convince their sphere of influence on the uniqueness and exclusivity of the Christian faith and ultimately, Jesus Christ our Lord.

> So Christ himself gave the apostles, the prophets, the
> evangelists, the pastors and teachers, to equip his people for
> works of service, so that the body of Christ may be built up until

we all reach unity in the faith and in the knowledge of the Son
of God and become mature, attaining to the whole measure of
the fullness of Christ.
Ephesians 4:11-13

Unity, knowledge, maturity — we stand UNDIVIDED. Jesus promised, if we gather in His name, he would be in the midst of us. How
often do we assemble to have church or a 'worship experience' but
forget to focus the gathering in 'His name'? The songs are a warm up
for the crowd to stroll in at their leisure and become acquainted to the
service. The offering is manipulated into a blessing if we participate
and a curse if we don't. Finally, the 3 point structurally inspired Greek
sermon is man-centered to build up to the level of being puffed up. If
Jesus was standing on the platform in our midst, how would we worship? If Jesus was standing on the platform during the preaching, what
would we say to center the message on Him? A Christ-centered message
is disregarded as too theo-
logical and uninteresting.
Instead, preference is
made for 'relevant practical teaching.' That is to
say, 'a message about
me and my life.' Barna

> Our fascination with church metrics
> refocuses our efforts to emphasize less
> on equipping the saints with truth and
> instead, encourage the attendees with
> life-coaching idealism.

Research shows that three-quarters of US adults (75%) say they are
looking for ways to live a more meaningful life.[13] Our monthly sermon
series reflects such an interest.

For I resolved to know nothing while I was with you except
Jesus Christ and him crucified.
1 Corinthians 2:2

The humanistic gospel is the core message of the evangelical
church. In our desperation to retain Christians, we compete with the
message of self-fulfillment, self-actualization and self-esteem which
saturates the marketplace of the leading influencers of culture which
George Barna made us aware of. The Church is as guilty as the congregation for their insidious love affair with themselves. Pastor Rod
Parsley sums it well, "Here in America we've taken a culture built upon

the blood and sweat of pioneers and gradually transformed it into the land of self-indulgent, self-absorbed, and self-aggrandizing." [14]

Popularity and comfortability is not what we settle for, it is what we strive for. Young adults have an inner felt need to be popular and famous. According to surveys, current young adults would rather be famous than rich. This need for acceptance and popularity is part of the social media, reality TV culture, which has taken the average person and made them unique, famous, and...above average. Increasingly, more students believe they are superstars! Dr. Keith Ablow believes we are raising a generation of deluded narcissists.[15]

Church Facebook Fan Pages and congregants' profile pages are starving for new 'friends' and 'followers.' There is no contentment when you are simply tolerated. We want to be generously celebrated. Not only were we warned about deception and hatred for truth in the days preceding Christ's coming, but also the worship of "self."

> People will be lovers of themselves...
> **2 Timothy 3:2**

In the book *Seven Faith Tribes*, George Barna defines the Casual Christian demographic. Over 80% of self-described Christians fall into this category.

- (Casual Christians) do not stir up conflict or controversy: such friction makes them uncomfortable... Casuals are tethered to a set of core values that dictate their behavior and attitudes, yet they remain very open to a wide array of moral perspectives and lifestyles. They do not consider this to be caving in to social pressure as much as satisfying their desire to get along with others and experiment with new options... They are prone to adopt nontraditional viewpoints in order to stay connected to other people and to remain at peace with their world. ... They have no particular passion about vocally representing God and His ways to the world. Casuals are more interested in living a simple, low-key life filled with happiness and fulfillment than pursuing faith based on truth and righteousness.

- Personal comfort is a major objective. Their life revolves around keeping peace with everyone: God, family, friends, neighbors, coworkers.

- They do not get excited about matters of faith.

- Less likely than other Americans to look forward to going to church services, reading the bible, discussing religion.

- They push the boundary of traditional Christian morality.

- Their highest priority in life is family.

- They do not believe absolute moral truth exists.

- They do support Christian symbols in public but also support homosexual marriage.

- Despite the fact that Casuals consider themselves to be Christian, almost universally own one or more Bibles and consider the Bible to be God's word and principles for humankind to live by, less than 2% have a biblical worldview.

- Less than 1 out of every three Casuals agree that success is about obedience to God rather than personal accomplishments in life.

- Mystically being guided by God and relying heavily upon their own skills and abilities, they must make sense out of the world — is perhaps the foundational spiritual reality that defines Casuals.

- The Christianity of the Casuals is a comfortable safety net for life...Religion is a private matter in their eyes, not something to be constantly talked about or aggressively shared with those whose lives have no direct connection with God. They read the Bible for solace more than instruction, and they take pleasure in its culturally accepted principles rather than admonition from its higher expectations of how to live.

The righteous foundation of our country is progressively collapsing under the weight of rebellion, lawlessness and deception. The Church has been negligent to raise up compassionate, contending, committed Christ-followers. Our teaching and training to equip and empower believers to reach their sphere of influence (since the church only owns 10% of the influence market) has been inadequate.

An alternative liberal form of Christianity has emerged with many young pastoral leaders riding its coattails to cultural acceptance and popularity. Pastor Michael Youssef, founder and President of Leading the Way Ministries, explains "Over time, liberal Christianity has developed a humanistic understanding of what the Christian faith is about. They claim that Christians who still believe the Bible is God's perfect self-revelation are stuck back in the first century. Society has evolved, they say. And because society has evolved, God must be evolving also. After all, why else would He allow such change to occur?" [16]

Commenting on the effect and the difference of Liberal Christianity, conservative film producer, Dinesh D'Souza, says "Liberal Christians assume a kind of reverse mission. Instead of being the churches' missionaries to the world, they become the world's missionaries to the church... A small but influential segment of liberal Christianity rejects all the central doctrines of Christianity. H. Richard Niebuhr famously summed up their credo "The God without wrath, brought men without sin, into a kingdom without judgement, to the ministrations of a Christ without a cross." [17]

Recalling the chilling downward trends of a simple biblical worldview, together with the rise of liberal Christianity, experts who study the sociological leanings declared, "During the string of retrospectives that greeted the new year, many named 2013 the year of a progressive renaissance. From the continued rise of the religiously unaffiliated, to the progress of marriage equality as a political and cultural force, and the election of Bill de Blasio, many observers have suggested we're entering a new and more liberal era: The old ideas have been tried, found wanting, and Americans are now ready to discard them, we've been told." [18]

Radical liberalism has redefined and removed traditional morality. The bedrock of Western morality is rooted in the Judeo-Christian Bible. In navigating their attempt to make a new secular world, they relentlessly challenged, defamed and twisted the Christian scriptures to portray hatred, intolerance and an unscientific, unreasonable, religious worldview. They criticize and condemn the 5 Core Beliefs of a Christian worldview and try to censure and shut down the public speech or the public education of these beliefs. In Section III, The UNDIVIDED will overindulge you with the well known resistance towards the Christian faith and our core beliefs.

In Robert Bork's book, *Slouching Towards Gomorrah*, he intelligently explained radical liberalism's set ideological goals of radical individualism (removal of moral restraints) and radical egalitarianism (guaranteed equal outcome, not merely opportunity). He noticed America was slouching or trending downward towards an era of anti-biblical reasoning and hatred towards traditional moral beliefs and boundaries. Bork says, "The structures of society — Family, Business, Church, Education is being attacked and losing its influence while the State [government] is being enhanced. Liberalism wants to move away from the conformed society but it has not replaced the success pattern. This creates individuals who want to fulfill every inner desire without moral limits and yet still enjoy the prosperity and success that the pillars of society create." [19]

I assume I have not belabored the point. We will either bury the Bible in a secular, socialist, humanist, atheist grave as Pallbearers, or bear the burden of Paul the Apostle, as Paul-bearers, and turn our world upside down by reversing the trend of biblical unbelief.

The Christian faith is on the decline and the opposing anti-biblical worldview is on the rise. The Church cannot abandon our moral responsibility to teach and love as the salt and light of the world. Too often we have succumbed to the pressure of popular opinion to 'preach the gospel and use words if necessary.' Sounds religious. Sounds spiritual. Sounds humble. It's completely unbiblical and a dangerous practice to follow.

Jesus was admired and respected for the good works He did. His miracles and selfless service left even His enemies speechless without accusation. Nevertheless, he was hated and despised.

"We are not stoning you for any good work," they replied, "but for blasphemy, because you, a mere man, claim to be God."
John 10:33

Face the facts, the Church, when faithful to the command of Christ to 'go into all the world and preach the gospel' will be hated and persecuted for the truth which we speak. We can endlessly feed the poor and free human trafficking victims, but despite that, we will not be applauded or welcomed on the stage of a secular liberal culture. To be tolerated in our culture, we do not need to change the perception about Christianity, we need to forsake the biblical Christ. The stumbling block of offense.

"Blessed is anyone who does not stumble
on account of me."
Matthew 11:6

This generation is desperate for the Paul-bearers to find their fortitude and moral strength to speak up in the vain of the apostles and prophets. The Bible was written in the loneliness of their rejection with their blood-stained, persecuted bodies. The early church fathers preserved the scriptures through their blood. The mystics and monks preserved it through self denial and humility. John Wycliffe and Martin Luther put the Bible in the language of the people under intense persecution and resistance. Are we the generation that will prepare its resting place in Western Civilization, as it searches to find growth and renewed love for its timeless truths in the developing world?

Christ said the gates of hell will not prevail (Matthew 16:18). By literal implications, hell is on the defense with gates to hold us back. The Church is on the offense expanding God's dominion on earth. As we view the global Church, indeed, we find a last day revival shaking nations and cultures of various tribes and tongues. Our geographical hemispheres are different but so are the spiritual atmospheres. They suffer persecution and tribulation while boldly living out their faith under Islamic regimes, Communist governments and extreme poverty. The burden of Paul is heavy, but the blessings of God are heavenly!

For our light and momentary troubles are achieving for us an
eternal glory that far outweighs them all.
2 Corinthians 4:17

As Paul-bearers, we must live nearly the identical Christian lifestyle as the Apostle Paul. He had a reputation of being a 'fool,' scorned and mocked by the intellectual elites, threatened by his religious counterparts and imprisoned by business owners for wrecking their profit and prized possession of a soothsaying young girl. Society was against him but the Spirit was for him. He had a brand that was recognizable. When the general public thought of him, the first thing that came to their head to describe him was "out of his mind."

If we are "out of our mind," as some say, it is for God…
2 Corinthians 5:13

He was truly following Christ, as our Savior had the same reputation.

When his (Jesus) family heard about this,
they went to take charge of him, for they said,
"He is out of his mind."
Mark 3:21

As Christ, Paul rejected something of more value in the eyes of the world. His education, status and pride became secondary or nonexistent after his encounter with Jesus. Just as Christ became a man and set aside His heavenly authority and glory to embrace the suffering and rejection of His own people, Paul too, laid aside the prestige and position of a highly respected Pharisee to embrace the suffering and rejection from his people. As Paul-bearers, we must lay aside popularity and community positions to faithfully preach the gospel of Jesus Christ.

But whatever were gains to me I now consider loss for the sake of Christ. What is more, I consider everything a loss because of the surpassing worth of knowing Christ Jesus my Lord, for whose sake I have lost all things. I consider them garbage, that I may gain Christ and be found in him, not having a righteousness of my own that comes from the law, but that which is through faith in Christ—the righteousness that comes from God on the basis of faith. I want to know Christ—yes, to know the power of his resurrection and participation in his sufferings, becoming like him in his death, and so, somehow, attaining to the resurrection from the dead.
Philippians 3:7-11

The 'out of his mind' Apostle sacrificed the pleasures of this world in exchange for the persecution from the worldly. Surely, we can reverse this trend of biblical unbelief if we forfeit our fame and fortunes to preach the holy faith given to us.

Are they servants of Christ? (I am out of my mind to talk like this.) I am more. I have worked much harder, been in prison more frequently, been flogged more severely, and been exposed to death again and again.
2 Corinthians 11:23

Dear friends, although I was very eager to write to you about the salvation we share, I felt compelled to write and urge you to contend for the faith that was once for all entrusted to God's holy people.
Jude 3

The falling away from the faith has begun. Lawlessness is rampant. Truth is vilified. Wickedness is mainstream. Sin is regarded as religious rhetoric which manipulates and controls the morally unrestrained evolved man, who has been predetermined by his genetics and environment to fulfill every inner desire. The 5 Core Beliefs of the Christian faith are under assault. Young adults feel ashamed for the biblical claims of exclusivity and absolute truth as they have been indoctrinated through a pluralistic public school system, hostile to religious expression.

As Pallbearers, we will carry the Bible to its humanistic grave. As Paul-bearers, we will carry the burden and prepare the way of the Lord with Spirit-empowered boldness. Martin Lloyd Jones, the minister at Westminster Chapel in London for over 30 years who studied revival, stood for truth and strongly opposed Liberal Christianity said, "Any study of church history, and particularly any study of the great periods of revival or reawakening, demonstrates above everything else just this one fact: that the Christian Church during all such periods has spoken with authority. The great characteristic of all revivals has been the authority of the preacher."

Chapter Two

Absence of Accountability

"...when the Son of Man comes, will he find faith on the earth?"
Luke 18:8

And the Lord's servant must not be quarrelsome but must
be kind to everyone, able to teach, not resentful. Opponents
must be gently instructed, in the hope that God will grant them
repentance leading them to a knowledge of the truth, and that
they will come to their senses and escape from the trap of the
devil, who has taken them captive to do his will.
2 Timothy 2:24-26

...what may be known about God is plain to them,
because God has made it plain to them.
For since the creation of the world God's invisible qualities—
his eternal power and divine nature—have been clearly seen,
being understood from what has been made, so that people
are without excuse. For although they knew God, they neither
glorified him as God nor gave thanks to him, but their thinking
became futile and their foolish hearts were darkened. Although
they claimed to be wise, they became fools...
Romans 1:19-22

In 1947, Roswell, New Mexico was the object of an intense UFO investigation. Supposedly, an extra-terrestrial aircraft with alien occupants crashed in a nearby field 75 miles away. To this day, conspiracy theories run rampant of a classified government coverup. Somewhere deep inside Area 51 are friends from another galaxy. Former President Bill Clinton admitted his belief in the existence of aliens on Jimmy Kimmel Live. Clinton said, "If we were visited someday I wouldn't be surprised...I just hope it's not like 'Independence Day.' It may be the only way to unite this increasingly divided world of ours ... think about how all the differences among the people of Earth would seem small if we felt threatened by a space invader." [1] Roswell tourism still runs high as alien hunters journey in faith. There is no proof. There is no evidence. Only blind faith and hopeful assumptions. Per G. K. Chesterton, the great British writer and Christian apologist, "Those that fail to believe in God, do not believe in nothing, but believe in anything." Aliens top the list. Decide, Roswell or Resurrection — which requires more faith?

According to the famous cosmologist, Carl Sagan, there is a fascinating probability that aliens exist or did exist at one time. God, not so much...? The Drake Equation, developed in 1961, tries to quantify the number of advanced civilizations in our galaxy. In theory, the number should be high, but in reality there is no hint of life outside of earth. The reason for this, according to Sagan and others, is a final variable: the high probability that advanced civilizations destroyed themselves.[2] He asserts the search for intelligent extraterrestrial life is time well spent, though no signs, signals or radio waves exists. Sagan flatly rebuts the scientific, observable evidence that points to a complex universe brought into existence by an intelligent, extraordinary Creator. Carl Sagan remarks "As science advances there seems to be less and less for God to do... Whatever it is we cannot explain lately is attributed to God...And then after awhile, we will explain it, and so that's no longer God's realm." [3]

Sagan authoritatively claims in his *Cosmos* series, "The cosmos is all there is, all there was, and all there ever will be." His infamous ideology is now promoted to a new and less Bible-believing generation by Neil Degrasse Tyson in the 2014 edition of *Cosmos* on FOX. Sounding slightly blasphemous, he bluntly denied the existence of an everlasting God, as Jesus Christ claimed:

> "I am the Alpha and the Omega," says the Lord God, "who is, and who was, and who is to come, the Almighty."
> **Revelation 1:8**

Sagan is a highly respected scientist. Though he passed away in 1996, he helped to spawn the current movement of aggressive atheism by his critical thoughts towards religion and the foolish notion of a spiritual world untraceable to the material world. He, among many others, triumphantly boast in the near sovereignty of science. Still, the best scientists struggle when explaining human consciousness or discovering the cure for most diseases. There is much to be learned, more advancements to be made and most questions are still to be answered. However, the greatest question and the easiest to answer, 'Does God Exist?' is flippantly attacked and critically dismantled as rubbish by leading scientists. This is not due to empirical evidence but the widely held assumption that "The cosmos [material world] is all there is, all there was, and all there ever will be." This is the worldview of materialism or naturalism. The immaterial world is imaginable, but not practical, since it is not physical.

Here is Harvard biologist Richard Lewontin:

"We take the side of science in spite of the patent absurdity of some of its constructs, in spite of its failure to fulfill many of its extravagant promises of health and life, in spite of the tolerance of the scientific community for unsubstantiated just-so stories, because we have a prior commitment — a commitment to materialism. It is not that the methods and institutions of science somehow compel us to accept a material explanation of the phenomenal world, but, on the contrary, that we are forced by our prior commitment to material causes to create an apparatus of investigation and a set of concepts that produce material explanations, no matter how counter-intuitive, no matter how mystifying to the uninitiated. Moreover, that materialism is absolute, for we cannot allow a Divine Foot in the door." [4]

The above is a pure and undefiled admission to the true sprit of modern science.

No matter what the evidence, we have a commitment to our prior assumption — there is no God.

Kansas City University Professor SC Todd, agrees with biologist Lewontin, "Even if all the data pointed to an intelligent designer, such a hypothesis is excluded from science because it is not naturalistic."[5] Scientists are not searching for answers, they are satisfied in their assumptions.

A worldview is like a nose or ego, everyone has one, but some are more noticeable than others. There is a movement of aggressive atheism which is not satisfied to keep God out of their materialistic worldview. They want their worldview to be noticed, along with their egos, as having the

> No matter what the evidence, we have a commitment to our prior assumption — there is no God.

final authoritative answer above faith and religion. In chapter 3, I will explain in more detail the materialistic or naturalistic worldview. In short, there is no spirit realm. Everything comes from a natural and evolved universe with no supernatural origin. According to Dean Hamer's book *The God Gene: How Faith Is Hardwired into Our Genes,* God was created by man due to genetic mutations in the evolutionary process.

Conservative writer and film producer, Dinesh D'Souza, spotlights the vigorous undertaking by leading scientific atheists to destroy religion in his book *What's So Great About Christianity*. According to D'Souza "The distinguishing element of modern atheism is its intellectual militancy and moral self-confidence. We have seen a spate of atheist books in recent years, like Richard Dawkins's *The God Delusion*, Sam Harris's *The End of Faith*, Victor Stenger's *God: The Failed Hypothesis*, and Christopher Hitchens's *God Is Not Great*. Other writers, like E.O. Wilson, Carl Sagan, Daniel Dennett, and Steven Pinker have also weighed in with anti-religious and anti-Christian tracts. In Europe, the Wall Street Journal reports, philosopher Michael Onfray has rallied the unbelievers with his bestselling *Atheist Manifesto*, which posits a "final battle" against the forces of Christianity." [6] Onfray states emphatically,

> "we must fight for a post-Christian secularism, that is to say atheistic, militant, and radically opposed to...Western Judeo-Christianity...[7]

These author names and their vehement anti-religious themed books may not be familiar to the average Christian. Nonetheless, their influence is extremely high on the belief systems of young adults. Less than 1% of them have a biblical worldview. These leading atheists directly influence the teaching of science and philosophy in top universities. By so doing, they indirectly build a materialistic worldview on impressionable students who are unprepared for such critical thought and claims against the idea of God and the beauty of religious faith. Surveys pinpoint thirteen million confessed atheists in our God blessed America. In congruence, 30% of adults under 30 years of age claim to have 'no religious faith.' [8]

Why are these numbers climbing at alarming rates? Richard Dawkins has a part to play in this symphony of religious destruction. Larry Taunton, apologist and President of Fixed Point Ministries, describes the influence of Dawkins "Atheism is becoming a political force. Richard Dawkins is the new Pat Robertson of Atheism." [9] Dawkins's book, *The God Delusion* is the #1 Atheist book of all time. He was the host of the British TV program *The Virus of Faith*, where he compared Moses to Hitler and described teaching children religion as 'child abuse.' To quote Dawkins's view of religion "The great unmentionable evil at the center of our culture is monotheism. From a barbaric Bronze Age text known as the Old Testament, their anti-human religions have evolved: Judaism, Christianity, and Islam." [10] In 2006, he informed the *Sunday Times* that he was setting up a charity to "divert donations from the hands of 'missionaries' and church based charities because the enlightenment is under threat. So is reason. So is truth. So is science." [11]

He also proudly contributed to the DVD, *The God That Wasn't There*, which you or your loved ones can receive for free by logging into www.blasphemychallenge.com. Requirement: deny the Father, the Son and the Holy Spirit using your selfie webcam or smartphone. My deepest apologies, all 1001 promotional DVD's have already been distributed. The response was overwhelming.

Those other unfamiliar atheist authors and scientific voices do not fare much better in their loathing opinion towards faith and religion. Steven Weinberg writes "Anything that we scientists can do to weaken the hold of religion should be done and may in the end be our greatest contribution to civilization." Sam Harris, in *The End of Faith,* condemns what he terms "the lunatic influence of religious belief." Christopher Hitchens states "All religions and all churches are equally demented in their belief in divine intervention, divine intercession, or even the existence of the divine in the first place." [12] In addition, Texas Tech biology professor Michael Dini, refuses to write letters of recommendation for top students for admittance in medical school if they believe in God. Dr. James Brink, the university's assistant provost, supported Dini. "I think a student with a strong faith and belief in creationism should not attend a public university, but rather should attend a biblically grounded university where their ideas are reinforced instead of scientifically challenged." [13]

"we must fight for a post-Christian secularism, that is to say atheistic, militant, and radically opposed to...Western Judeo-Christianity...

The denial of God has expanded beyond science, education and politics. It has found a new frontier and thrives with unprecedented results — an atheist church. The Sunday Assembly's first meeting was on January 6, 2013, in the city of London. The two founders were actually comedians; Sanderson Jones and Pippa Evans. Their vision and motto was quite unique for your non-typical Sunday morning non-religious gathering. In a sense of wonder, delight and bewilderment, they attributed their non-supernatural growth to these attractive simple values, clear message and excellent mission.

- We are a godless congregation that celebrates life.
- We have an awesome motto: Live Better, Help Often and Wonder More.
- A super mission: to try to help everyone find and fulfill their full potential.
- An awesome vision: a godless congregation in every town, city, or village that wants one.[14]

Currently, there are twenty-eight godless, atheist congregations around the globe under the 'non-spiritual covering' of the Sunday Assembly. Imagine, one church multiplying to twenty-eight church plants in less than 18 months, with a trajectory rising to nearly one hundred congregations by the end of 2014. Within the first nine months of their existence, they experienced a 3000% growth rate! "The 3,000 percent growth rate might make this non-religious Assembly the fastest growing church in the world," organizers boast.[15]

Atheism just had their day of Pentecost!

Can we blame professional comics for originating the Atheist Church? If you took away our two hour weekly church attendance, is there any difference between us as Christians and the average atheist in:

1. What we say...
2. What we watch...
3. What we listen to...
4. Where we go...
5. What we wear...

As Western Civilization further withdraws itself from the shadow of God's wings, we need to seriously consider the leftovers of 2,000 years of Christian influence within mainstream culture. For instance, holidays. What would our school calendars and shopping circulars be without St. Valentine's Day or St. Patrick's Day?

There is no need to fret. Our liberal virtuoso political leaders have an innovative idea, National Darwin Day.

Atheism just had their day of Pentecost!

On January 26, 2014, NJ Representative, Rush Holt, from District 12, introduced into the US House of Representatives a resolution, H.Res. 467, to designate February 12, 2014, as "Darwin Day" in recognition of the 205th anniversary of Charles Darwin's birth. Rep Holt, "To me, Charles Darwin is even more than the author of the theory of evolution, as great as that is. He represents a way of thinking, a philosophy, a methodology. It was his thirst for knowledge and his scientific approach to discovering new truths that enabled him to develop the theory of evolution. This lesson, about the value of scientific thinking, is almost as valuable as the theory he uncovered." [16]

This is not some weird quirk originating from NJ or even limited to a Congressional proposal. This, as the Sunday Assembly, is an international sensation. Darwin Day is a British invention, begun not long after the scientist's death in 1882. The first large, formalized gatherings occurred in 1909 with celebrations in London, New York and New Zealand. Modern methods of celebration and community events include: Zazzle and Cafe Press offering Darwin Day cards. Samples: "I naturally select you" and "Let's evolve together." Can Hallmark be far behind? According to the International Darwin Day Foundation, over 90 groups of atheists, humanists and other freethinkers are holding local celebrations that run from potluck dinners (the so-called phylum feasts) to nature outings, lectures, book discussions and film screenings. [17]

It would be repetitive and meaningless to list the ongoing legal challenges from atheists groups to remove "God" from the Pledge of Allegiance, War Memorial crosses from public lands and The Ten Commandments from public displays. Equally repetitive would be to list mocking religious videos from Lady Gaga and statements from HBO's Bill Maher, who received the 2009 Richard Dawkins award from Atheist Alliance International. It is common knowledge and well documented. There is a movement to silence Christian religious expression, as other anti-religious voices use their fields of expertise to defame God and debunk Christianity. It is a Saul Alinsky method of madness and manipulation. Demonize Christianity and demoralize Christians. Slowly and steadily, each generation is becoming assimilated into a secular culture, leaving behind cherished traditions, values and eternal doctrine.

> There is no need to fret. Our liberal virtuoso political leaders have an innovative idea, National Darwin Day.

Why is there such vent up anger towards the theory of God's existence and more so, God's involvement in the day to day operations of our world? We will continually discover throughout this book, and have already revealed, the dogmatic assumption by atheists that there is no god, even if evidence would contradict their firmly held religious belief. Atheists, whether influenced by the scientific community or the disappointment of personal tragedy, have common objections to God's existence; distinctly categorized into moral absolutes and evil.

Societies void of moral restraints are historically non-theistic or non-monotheistic cultures. Pluralistic and pagan empires have celebrated man's lust and human sexuality proportionally balanced by violence. Atheists unduly want to be their own god, doing their own thing.

The fool says in his heart, "There is no God." They are corrupt, their deeds are vile; there is no one who does good.
Psalm 14:1

The context of the word fool, often used in the Old Testament, denotes one who is morally deficient. The Psalm justly reads, 'no one' does good. I am identical to the unbelieving atheist in my own sin-ful nature. Having said that, I am different in my righteous position in Christ. My moral deficiency, through the great exchange of Christ's blood purchasing me from the slave market of sin, has been trans-formed into a moral surplus — the righteousness of Jesus Christ. The atheist continues to play the fool, a role often preferred for personal pleasure and exploration. Today's atheist or fool is naturally intelligent while spiritually deficient. Allow me to explain.

I defer once again to the spokesperson of modern unbelief, Richard Dawkins, who has unkindly said "The God of the Old Testa-ment is arguably the most unpleasant character in all fiction: jealous and proud of it, a petty, unjust, unforgiving control freak, a vindictive, bloodthirsty ethnic cleanser, a misogynistic, homophobic, racist, infan-ticidal, genocidal, filicidal, pestilential, megalomaniacal, sadomasoch-istic, capriciously malevolent bully." [18] His excessive, savage criticism of God is a radical dispute of God's judgement and moral control. He, among many, prefer a god who has no standards and fundamentally no purpose for humanity. Hence, materialism often leads to nihilism.

The Apostle Paul quoted the previous mentioned Psalm 14, in the third chapter of Romans. He incorporated the following in the epistle:

There is no fear of God before their eyes.
Psalm 36:1

The morally deficient 'fool' denies God because he has no fear of God. His lack of fear is the rebellious dissension against any form of judgement. "The fear of God is not the beginning of wisdom. The fear of God is the death of wisdom," said famed Attorney Clarence Darrow, who fervently led the legal team for John Scopes in the 1925 Scopes Monkey Trial for teaching evolution in the public school. He also be-lieved in man's genetics and environment as predetermined factors which made free will and moral decisions unbearable and impossible for some 'evolved' humans to live up to, as he defended the teenage thrill killers Leopold and Loeb in 1924. During a speech in Toronto in 1930, Darrow stated "I believe that religion is the belief in future life and in God. I don't believe in either. I don't believe in God as I don't believe in Mother Goose." Even upon his death he was quoted in his eulogy by Emanuel Haldeman-Julius, "I am an Agnostic because I am not afraid to think. I am not afraid of any god in the universe who would send me or any other man or woman to hell. If there were such a being, he would not be a god; he would be a devil." May the reader take note, Darrow started the American Civil Liberties Union, the non profit organization that for the past 50 years has focused heavily on removing God from the public square and the public school.

Atheism is not the flourishing repercussion of a technologically advanced, enlightened world. Men for millennium have denied the existence of judgement or one eternal creator holding all men accountable. Inevitably, these cultures corrupted and the judgement which was denied was no longer delayed. Noah's world had the flood, Pharaoh's world had the plagues, the Roman Empire had the Goths and Barbarians. America, according to Rabbi Jonathan Cahn, in his book *The Harbinger: The Ancient Mystery That Holds the Secret of America's Future*, will also find its reckoning day.

Morality is a major emphasis of Section II, The Core Belief. For atheists, it is the underlying assumption which makes their system of belief attractive to a sexually indulgent culture. Non-judgement eases the corrupt conscience allowing the immoral to become normal. Atheism is more popular than the unguided natural selection of evolution. Only 14% of Americans believe God had no part in human existence. [19] Empirical evidence is not the reason Atheism will overtake Christianity in 30-40 years. The fatal flaw is the unwarranted pursuit as Robert Bork puts it in *Slouching Towards Gomorrah*, to increase the 'space between the walls.' In other words, more moral liberty, less moral restraints.

Only a materialistic view, which in actuality is an atheist view of the existence of God, lends itself to the practicality of living in a world with no moral absolutes and no pending judgement. It is attractive and it is anti-Christian.

For the time will come when people will not
put up with sound doctrine. Instead, to suit their own desires,
they will gather around them a great number of teachers
to say what their itching ears want to hear.
They will turn their ears
away from the truth and turn aside to myths.
2 Timothy 4:3-4

There are many lies, many temptations and many false religions. The rejection of sound doctrine and the receiving of demonic doctrine is rampant. What is the dogmatic doctrine of the devil? Simple: 'You will be as god. You will know good from evil.'

God becomes a deistic figure far removed from the new 'god of this world,' humanity (Satan is the actual 'god of this world,' humanity presumes it is them). Man increases the space between the walls; no moral limits or eternal consequences. Man alone decides good from evil.

Final point, evil. Atheists not only use science, but reason to disqualify God from being acknowledged. With the expanded space between the walls, they claim moral equality or superiority over the devout religious disciple. Science and reason has without debate led to the betterment of society. Medicine and inventions have produced a higher quality of life. They glorify in their self-claimed contributions while hypocritically 'judging' dishonorable and despicable religious corruption and wrongdoing.

> Only a materialistic view, which in actuality is an atheist view of the existence of God, lends itself to the practicality of living in a world with no moral absolutes and no pending judgement. It is attractive and it is anti-Christian.

Sam Harris calls religion "the most potent source of human conflict, past and present." [20] The Crusades, The Inquisition, The Religious Reformation Wars and The Salem Witch Trials all blamed the scapegoat of Christianity. Philosopher Bertrand Russell concurs in *Why I Am Not a Christian* "there was every kind of cruelty practiced upon all sorts of people in the name of religion." [21]

One, if the idea of God is simply a genetic mutation in the evolutionary process, do not blame religion for evil, blame genetics! This has become the normal default legal defense of liberal attorneys anyway. Second, if each generation corporately decides moral boundaries and redefines moral restraints and standards, then is it not the height of arrogance and intolerance to judge our modern world in comparison to those living in centuries past? If there is no universal moral principle which applies to all men at all times, then how can we fairly apply our view of religious pluralism in contrast to their more exclusive view?

Further still, religion has contributed more good in a dissimilar proportion to secularism and atheism. In regard to the evil of religion:

- The original Crusade was a response to the prior Islamic conquering of Christian holy lands around Palestine, including Jerusalem.

- The Crusaders were pilgrims, not conquerors. Most (not all) returned to Europe poorer than when they left.

- Christians wanted to defend themselves from further Islamic advancement and the conquering of Christian Europe.

- The Inquisition was persecution of Christians by other Christians. Most of the guilty were sentenced to penance, fasting or service. Sadly, in the end, around 3,000 were unjustly executed over a period of 350 years. *Note — over 3,000 children are aborted each day in America.

- The Jews, sorrowfully, did suffer. However, not simply because they were Jewish, but because after King Ferdinand and Queen Isabella expelled them from Spain, many remained and assimilated into Christianity. These 'new Christians' were not viewed as true converts. Christians persecuted confessed 'christians.'

- The Religious European Wars, historians explain, were far more about land, territory and wealth than the proper way to worship. In essence, these were national wars for national dominance.

- Salem Witch Trials, were justly blamed for religious persecution. A total of 19 people were executed in the name of God. A few more died in captivity.

Overall, the sum of death in the name of God tallies around the fifteen million mark in 2,000 years of religious wars. Even more mind-blowing is the multiplied sum of 120 million deaths in less than one hundred years of twentieth century secular and communist regimes. Philosopher Friedrich Nietzsche saw this sinister slant of organized political men unrestrained by the fear and judgement of God. He predicted that the next two centuries would be cataclysmic, with wars and violence beyond all imagining. The death of God, Nietzsche wrote, would result in the total eclipse of all values. Since values no longer came from God, they would now be made up by man.[22]

Charles Krauthammer writes of the observation by Arthur Schlesinger (and others) that, "The declining faith in the supernatural has been accompanied by the rise of the monstrous totalitarian creeds of the 20th century." [23] Man caused more destruction through atheist regimes and conquest than religious zealots ever cruelly imagined. Even natural disasters lack the equivalence of loss of life compared to the atheistic communist governments. Charles Krauthammer again comments "God cannot match the cruelty of his creation. For every Santorini [natural disaster] there are a hundred massacres of innocents. And that is the work of man — more particularly, the work of politics, of groups of men organized to gain and exercise power." [24]

Ironically, we overlook the horror which occurred in recent history while incessantly repeating the religious failures of generations far removed. Dinesh D'Souza points out, "Five hundred years after the Inquisition, we are still talking about it, but less than two decades after the collapse of "godless Communism," there is an eerie silence about the mass graves of the Soviet Gulag.[25]

Psalm 14 and Romans 3 begins to take on a more relevant hermeneutic meaning!

The fool says in his heart, "There is no God."
They are corrupt, their deeds are vile;
there is no one who does good.
Psalm 14:1

There is no one righteous, not even one;
there is no one who understands;
there is no one who seeks God.
All have turned away, they have together become worthless;
there is no one who does good, not even one.
Their throats are open graves, their tongues practice deceit.
The poison of vipers is on their lips.
Their mouths are full of cursing and bitterness.
Their feet are swift to shed blood;
ruin and misery mark their ways,

and the way of peace they do not know.
There is no fear of God before their eyes.
Romans 3:11-18

With mutual unbiased criticism, I expounded on the worse moments of 2,000 years of Christian history and the woeful wars of godless government. With restrained humility, I must brag on the goodness of the dignity and equality of life the Christian Church has initiated and advanced throughout Western Civilization. Mark Tooley writes in *Christianity Is Not Going Away*, "Christendom indeed has included nearly all the faults alleged, but it did not invent any of them. Theocracy, conquest, empire, slavery and hypocrisy have been intrinsic to nearly all human history. What the critics forget is that Christendom also refined the social conscience and capacity for reform to challenge its own moral failures. Christendom developed human rights and legal equality, social tolerance, constitutional democracy, free enterprise, technology, modern science and medicine, new levels of arts and literature, and refined notions of charity." [26] Atheists do not deny our contribution, but egotistically state that the 'Golden Age' of Christian influence is long gone and hopefully buried in their secular, humanistic, atheist grave. Apologist Larry Taunton, "Secularists and Atheists admit that Christianity gave us literature, arts, hospitals, social justice; but they also acknowledge what the Greek philosophers gave us — their view, thank you for what you did, but we can move on now." [27] For the Christian, God is not dead. For the atheist, God is extinct.

> Man unrestrained by religion defaults to a Darwinian logic with the lust to dominate their environment and natural foes, ushering in a "godless" twentieth century of ill-forgotten torture and human rights violations.

The unblessed hope of aggressive atheism is for the world to snuff out Christianity and 'move on.' Using pseudo science and the sins of religion, they adamantly criticize, critique and challenge Christian thought. Their science, as we will uncover in the Core Belief section, points indirectly to an absolute undeniable creator. The sins of religion, though harmful to the cause of Christ, work against their hypothesis.

Man unrestrained by religion defaults to a Darwinian logic with the lust to dominate their environment and natural foes, ushering in a "godless" twentieth century of ill-forgotten torture and human rights violations.

The seductive allure of Atheism, so attractive to fallen humanity, is the moral liberty to live a life without boundaries and without judgment. The vain and lustful glory of the here and now, to satisfy the decadent fool who shamefully says, "There is no god."

Chapter Three

Wrong Side of History

I tell you this so that no one may deceive you by
fine-sounding arguments… See to it that no one takes you
captive through hollow and deceptive philosophy, which
depends on human tradition and the elemental spiritual
forces of this world rather than on Christ.
Colossians 2:4,8

In fact, everyone who wants to live a godly life in Christ Jesus
will be persecuted, while evildoers and impostors will go from
bad to worse, deceiving and being deceived. But as for you,
continue in what you have learned and have become convinced
of, because you know those from whom you learned it,…
2 Timothy 3:12-14

The weapons we fight with are not the weapons of the world. On
the contrary, they have divine power to demolish strongholds.
We demolish arguments and every pretension that sets itself
up against the knowledge of God, and we take captive every
thought to make it obedient to Christ.
2 Corinthians 10:4-5

Hollywood hit the mark with, *Gravity,* a remarkable film and thrill
ride for the senses. The images were profoundly surreal with a
backdrop of earth's atmosphere and awe-inspiring, visual angles.
The spectacular view which astronaut Matt Kowalsky, played by George
Clooney, and Dr. Stone, played by Sandra Bullock, had of the world was

about to become hectic and hell-like. Their world view quickly turned reckless as their foundation was no longer attached to a solid structure.

"Explorer's been hit! Explorer, do you read? Explorer, over! Explorer! Astronaut is off structure, Dr. Stone is off structure!" Dr. Ryan Stone: "What do I do?" Matt Kowalsky: "Dr. Stone, detach. You must detach. If you don't detach that arm's going to carry you too far. Listen to my voice. You need to focus. I'm losing visual of you. In three-seconds, I won't be able to track you. You need to detach. I can't see you anymore. Do it now!"

Moments later, the hunt began for Dr. Stone in near-earth orbit. She randomly and uncontrollably was caught in an undisciplined spin. Possessing a distorted and undetectable view of the world, she none-theless, still had a view of the world. It was merely unexplainable.

Matt Kowalsky: "Houston, I've lost visual with Dr. Stone. Houston, I've lost visual of Dr. Stone... Do you copy?" Dr. Ryan Stone: "Yes, yes, I've detached." Matt Kowalsky: "Give me your position." Dr. Ryan Stone: "I don't know. I don't know. I'm spinning. I can't, I can't."

Dr. Stone could not, and neither can most Christians, accurately describe their worldview. The term *worldview* has nothing to do with the visual picture of your immediate physical surroundings. It has to do with your assumptions of the world, not the angles of the earth.

Our worldview is closely related to that which is experienced in the scene from *Gravity*. Aimlessly and without clear direction, we are floating from one worldview to another, unable to describe and define our actual location in the wide range of beliefs and opinions. Why? Because we have become detached from the solid, supporting structure of our biblical foundation, the gospel of Jesus Christ.

"Therefore everyone who hears these words of mine and puts
them into practice is like a wise man who built his house on
the rock. The rain came down, the streams rose, and the winds
blew and beat against that house; yet it did not fall, because it
had its foundation on the rock. But everyone who hears these
words of mine and does not put them into practice is like a
foolish man who built his house on sand. The rain came down,
the streams rose, and the winds blew and beat against that
house, and it fell with a great crash."
Matthew 7:24-27

"When the foundations are being destroyed,
what can the righteous do?"
Psalm 11:3

Foundations are important and necessary. Every home and life is built either on stone or sand. The foundation will either cause the home to stand erect for ages or collapse with ease in tense situations. If the foundation is destroyed, or if we become detached, as in *Gravity*, due to the shooting debris of persecution and pressure, then we will become lost in space as individual, moral agents and corporately as a collective society. In all seriousness, our life can be filled with beauty, wonder and personal achievements but if the foundation is weak or wicked, it will crack and the enemy of our soul will find his long awaited opportunity.

Ravi Zacharias, in Focus on the Family's *Truth Project* and as quoted in Rod Parsley's *Culturally Incorrect*, explained the unvarying constant of a stable, moral foundation by rehearsing a story of his visit to Columbus, OH.

I remember lecturing at Ohio State University. I was minutes away from beginning my lecture, and my host was driving me past a new building called the Wexner Center for Performing Arts. He said, "This is America's first postmodern building."

I was startled for a moment and I said, "What is a postmodern building?" He said, "Well, the architect said that he designed this building with no design in mind. When the architect was asked, 'Why?' he said, 'If life itself is capricious, why should our buildings have any design and any meaning?' So he has pillars that have no purpose. He has stairways that go nowhere. He has a senseless building built and somebody has paid for it."

I said, "So his argument was that if life has no purpose and design, why should the building have any design?" He said, "That is correct."

I then said, "Did he do the same with the foundation?" All of a sudden there was silence. You see, you and I can fool with the infrastructure as much as we would like, but we dare not fool with the foundation because it will call our bluff in a hurry." [1]

The words of Christ and biblical truth are not the absolute core of our foundation. Granted, even the stone and sand rest on hardened clay dirt deep within the ground. The real foundation which all things of faith and reason rest on is our worldview, otherwise known as our assumptions. You, me, everyone assumes some things to be true without cause or explanation. For example, I assume (believe) that God exists and He is involved in the universe and man's personal experience. The atheist assumes (believes) God does not exist. Neither hypothesis can be empirically proven but it is nearly impossible to sway the opposing person to leave their assumed position concerning the existence of God.

Before building our lives on the teachings of Christ, Christians must first assume that God does indeed exist. From this vantage point, we see a designed universe and life with purpose and divine value. The atheist, or forms of atheism intermingled in other world views, assumes God indeed does not exist. From their vantage point, they see an unexplainable, random world where human life is as valuable as the baby shrimp and butterfly from which we, through natural selection, evolved from. These diverse and mutually exclusive views of the world will undoubtedly lead to equally diverse opinions and beliefs on how humanity should order and manage themselves in this world. A world with God is the polar opposite of a world with no god.

What is a worldview and how important is it? According to www.colsoncenter.org, a leading worldview website, every person in history has asked themselves a few basic questions: 'Who am I?' 'Why am I here?' 'Is there a God?' 'What is the purpose of life?' Your answers to these questions make up your worldview — your set of beliefs about the nature of reality. But more importantly, because your worldview consists of your answers to the big questions, it determines your behavior in all areas of life — how you worship, how you relate to those around you, the way you study, how you work, how you use your abilities, the way you view sex, whether you get married, how you treat your spouse, the way you train your children, how you vote, the way you treat human life and even the way you deal with death. What's the bottom line? Your worldview is not only the most critical component of your thinking — it's the most critical component of your behavior. [2]

According to the American Heritage Dictionary, a worldview is "The overall perspective from which one sees and interprets the world.

A collection of beliefs about life and the universe held by an individual or a group." [3]

James Sire, in his book, *The Universe Next Door,* lists six questions which theologians and philosophers have discussed and rationalized for centuries. A worldview must be able to answer these, or such a worldview is insufficient and vague. Infallibly, our 5 Core Beliefs offer absolute answers to these struggling and annoying questions about our existence. Section II will cover these answers at length.

1. **What is the prime reality?**
   Core Belief: God is the creator and is sovereign over His creation.

2. **What is the nature of external reality?**
   Core Belief: God is the Creator and is sovereign over His creation.
   Core Belief: The devil is real and not merely a symbolic figure of evil.
   The world was created good, but evil entered the world through Satan, tempting Adam and Eve. Currently the world is cursed.

3. **What is a human being?**
   Core Belief: Man is sinful and saved by grace.
   Man became a living soul at creation, made in God's image, and currently in a fallen state, inherently sinful.

4. **What happens to a person at death?**
   Core Belief: Jesus is the sinless Savior, the Son of God.
   Forgiveness is granted, judgement rendered upon Christ, and eternal life is experienced.

5. **How do we know right from wrong?**
   Core Belief: The Bible is 100% true and its moral teachings apply today.

6. **What is the meaning of human history?**
   Core Belief: God is the Creator and is sovereign over His creation.
   Core Belief: Jesus is the sinless Savior, the Son of God.
   Core Belief: The Bible is 100% true and its moral teachings apply today.

Core Belief: The devil is real and not merely a symbolic figure of evil.

Core Belief: Man is sinful and saved by grace.

It is the Story of Creation, the Fall, the Redemption and the Consummation.

The following chart clarifies the difference of a biblical worldview compared to popular and influential opposing world views.

5 Core Beliefs

	Core Belief	Biblical Worldview	unBiblical Worldview
Creation	God is the Creator and Sovereign over His creation	Made in the image of God	Evolved from meaningless matter
Creation	God is the Creator and Sovereign over His creation	Valuable with purpose	Worthless, product of accident
Creation	The Bible is 100% true and its moral teachings apply today	Truth has been revealed to us	Truth has to be attained through experience
Creation	The Bible is 100% true and its moral teachings apply today	Objective Truth is God's moral standard	Truth is relative and personal
Fall	The devil is real, not merely symbolic of evil	Evil comes from within/ Temptation	Evil is a response to out-side influence/ Environment
Fall	Man is sinful and saved by grace	Man is Fallen and inherently sinful	Man is basically good
Fall	Man is sinful and saved by grace	Resist your sinful nature	Fulfill your inner desires
Redemption	Jesus is the sinless Savior, the Son of God	We need a savior	We can save ourselves
Redemption	Jesus is the sinless Savior, the Son of God	Faith in Christ liberates man	Religion is the chain that binds man

The mere thought that God exists and the possibility of reuniting with 'God,' 'higher power,' or 'universal consciousness,' is not a biblical worldview. As Christians, we are Theists — believe God is sovereign and involved in the affairs of men, but separate from His creation. The majority of Americans unknowingly are Deists — believe God exists, but far removed from everyday life.

Worldviews develop in childhood before the doctorate professor challenges one's faith. By the age of nine, the moral foundation and the reality of right and wrong has been formed. By age thirteen, the view of God and the universe has been formed.[4] Parents must become more pro-active in teaching and instilling a biblical worldview in their children. Relying upon Sunday School or youth groups to counteract and reeducate the misinformation children receive from TV, tablets and teachers is a forfeit of parental responsibility and a proven failed method.

A worldview is the starting point to logic and reason. The majority of worldviews have a glimpse of some truths, but none rest on absolute truth except for a biblical worldview. These opposing worldviews, as we will uncover, have a sense of brilliance and enlightenment. Therefore, intelligent and well-meaning individuals can logically disagree over a variety of issues and topics. Admirers and proponents of non-biblical worldviews have ideas and rational thoughts which sincerely reflect their education and experience all packaged in philosophical lingo. Both the believer and the unbeliever might have similar goals and hopes for humanity but come to extremely different versions of the path to achieve these goals and their human aspirations. Why? Their starting point, or their given assumption of basic unproven facts (God exists or does not exists) is different from the other.

When traveling to a certain location you need to know, not only your ending point but your starting point as well. Google Maps or any GPS system must know where you are coming from before it can accurately lead you to where you want to go. In other words, if you want to take your family to Washington D.C. the list of highways and turns from Trenton, NJ is absolutely unrelated to the highways and turns from Orlando, FL. If your starting point is wrong, the map cannot logically and successfully guide you to your intended destination. If our assumptions or worldview is wrong then, no matter how much logic, thought or reason is invested, we will inevitably arrive at an erroneous conclusion or the wrong destination.

Let us journey through time to the starting point when our assumptions became twisted and our relationship with God became tarnished. From here we can follow the path of opposing worldviews prevalent in our age.

> Now the serpent was more crafty than any of the wild animals the Lord God had made. He said to the woman, "Did God really say, You must not eat from any tree in the garden?"
> The woman said to the serpent, "We may eat fruit from the trees in the garden, but God did say, 'You must not eat fruit from the tree that is in the middle of the garden, and you must not touch it, or you will die.'" "You will not certainly die," the serpent said to the woman. "For God knows that when you eat from it your eyes will be opened, and you will be like God, knowing good and evil."
> **Genesis 3:1-4**

Theologically, we could recite countless sermons and life lessons which are evident in the Garden of Eden account. We discover a God who passionately pursued man even after man's act of treason and rebellion. A God who covered their sins and their bodies by sacrificing an animal because forgiveness is only made possible through the shedding of blood. The earth and mankind became cursed. The world became defunct and turned upside down. God offers hope with the promise of a savior and sentences the serpent to defeat and punishment. Behind the big picture of creation and the fall of man is the underlying theme and core belief of every unbiblical worldview. Man can be as 'god!'

It was a blasphemous exchange. Man became the center of his world. As his own god, man now reasoned that he alone could decide what is good and evil. The need to trust in God for such boundaries and absolute definitions was substituted for human knowledge. Man's mind was full of wonder and wretchedness. His ability to think was subject to his corrupt and fallen soul. But he was independent and as 'god,' he was now the center of his own world. Humanism has a long history!

There are two types of knowledge; revealed and attained. As the first humanists, Adam and Eve rejected God's instructions (revealed) for the new form of knowledge (attained). Revealed knowledge is available to men through the inspired and inerrant word of God. Attained knowledge is the kind of knowledge gained through education and experience. It gives mankind an uncanny sense of false peace and confidence in making decisions. Assumed beliefs are the starting points of a worldview. These lie outside of the realm of attained knowledge — unobtainable and unobservable. Humanity naturally prefers attained knowledge because it can be seen and touched. To observe and obey revealed knowledge is a walk of faith; not attractive or congruent to the fallen nature.

The Scriptures clearly lay out the consequences of man persistently living in a world managed by his acquired knowledge:

Ye shall not do after all the things that we do here this day,
every man whatsoever is right in his own eyes.
Deuteronomy 12:8 KJV

In those days there was no king in Israel, but every man did
that which was right in his own eyes.
Judges 17:6 KJV

Doing what is right in our own eyes seems to be a reoccurring and conventional error. As the 'gods' of this world attempt to resolve every moral, spiritual, political and financial dilemma without accessing God's revealed knowledge of Scripture, we are left frustrated as we're led to the brink of failure. Our good intentions and well-rounded education cannot logically guide us to our intended destination because our starting point, our worldview, our assumptions are wrong. C.S. Lewis says, "The most dangerous ideas in a society are not the ones that are being argued, but the ones that are being assumed?"

Do not be wise in your own eyes;
fear the Lord and shun evil.
Proverbs 3:7

The fear of the Lord is the beginning of wisdom,
and knowledge of the Holy One is understanding.
Proverbs 9:10

A biblical worldview starts at the fear of the Lord. Our under-standing of His wisdom and sovereignty gives us a credible foundation to build our lives and logically build our arguments for what is true and not true. An unbiblical worldview cannot discern what is good and evil because the god-like ability promised by Satan is a farce.

> The person without the Spirit does not accept the things that
> come from the Spirit of God but considers them foolishness,
> and cannot understand them because they are
> discerned only through the Spirit.
> **1 Corinthians 2:14**

To recap our journey thus far, a worldview is based on an assump-tion. That is your starting point of faith (i.e God exists/does not exists) and the point from which you build your reason and logic. Knowledge is required to eloquently and informatively build upon this foundation. However, there are two types of knowledge — what God has revealed and what man has attained. Some men assume God does exist but is not involved in this world (Diest). Some assume that God does not exist (Atheist). Both reject the revealed knowledge of God through the Holy Scriptures and do that which is right in his own eyes. This surely leads to a motley of opposing unbiblical worldviews. The Christian, a theist in contrast, assumes God is real and active in our world. This God has revealed truth and knowledge to us through the Bible, helping us to discern everything pertaining to life and godliness.

Your worldview is connected to your God-view. If your view of God is wrong, then how you understand and rationalize this world will be incorrect. A biblical worldview is a God-centered worldview — it's all about Him. All types of unbiblical worldviews are man-centered — it's all about us.

Now that we have a grasp on the tragedy of the Garden of Eden and man's humanistic replacement theology where man becomes a god, let us fast forward into our present world and the opposing world-views, the major founders, and their undue influence.

Adolf Hitler has been quoted saying, "If you tell a lie long enough, people will start to believe it." Ironically, that has played out over the years to be true! Humanity is more apt to believe a lie if the promise of such belief is worth the risk or reward. From snake oil salespeople, to used car lots, if you cunningly promise someone 'an offer they can't refuse,' they, with blind faith, will close the deal.

There has been and continues to be enemies of the gospel. These influencers of culture are deceived and are unwittingly used of the devil to deceive others in believing unbiblical worldviews based on false assumptions. Humanists, atheists, secularists and the like do not have a building or a weekly gathering. The Sunday Assembly, discussed in the previous chapter, is the exception; boasting a godless congregation. These worldviews and those who hold fast to them, do not seek first time visitors or follow up on new converts. They do not fund Community Family Days or intently live missional lives. Instead, they wage war by using the supremacy of the public schools, the public square and elected, public office. Forgive the pessimism but unquestionably, the Church has been outdone and outsmarted. The hearts and minds of our culture, along with many inside our congregations, have man-centered worldviews developed through the attained knowledge of the enlightenment. Without Christ, it is only natural to have such a view. The alarming trend is not the rejection of the gospel, but the assumption that God does not exist or His existence is not relevant to our world, our family, our life.

Most Americans nonchalantly say without pause, "God bless you," "God bless America," or "God help me." I could go further but that would be inappropriate. A vocal acknowledgement and mental assent to God can be, and most often is, intermingled in a practical atheist lifestyle. A person might claim to believe in God but when probed for their worldview through surveys, their belief is merely superficial. A biblical worldview has been substituted by: humanism, naturalism, statism and nihilism.

What are these worldviews and where or with whom did they originate? In 1770's-1790's, a major global shift would change the course of history and mark a significant revision of who is man and who is God. America, the new world start up and sovereign nation entrusted their fate and freedom to the foundations of religion and morality. These culturally unappreciated words were the motto the American founding fathers used to guarantee and sustain future liberty.

George Washington's Farewell Address Sept 17, 1796: "Religion and morality are an indispensable support...Religion and morality are necessary conditions of the preservation of free government."

John Adams, 2nd President 1776: "[I]t is religion and morality alone which can establish the principles upon which freedom can securely stand. The only foundation of a free constitution is pure virtue."

John Adams 1798: "[W]e have no government armed with power capable of contending with human passions unbridled by morality and religion... Our constitution was made only for a moral and religious people. It is wholly inadequate to the government of any other."

Benjamin Rush 1798, first surgeon general, started first anti slavery group: "The only foundation for a republic is to be laid in Religion. Without this there can be no virtue, and without virtue there can be no liberty."

Charles Carroll signer of Declaration of Independence, US Senator, 1800 letter to James McHenry: "Without morals a republic cannot subsist any length of time; they therefore who are decrying the Christian religion whose morality is so sublime and pure . . . are undermining the solid foundation of morals, the best security for the duration of free governments."

Samuel Adams Founding Father, organized Boston Tea Party, Governor of Massachusetts 1778: "Religion and good morals are the only solid foundation of public liberty and happiness."

Patrick Henry Governor of Virginia 1799: "Virtue, morality, and religion. This is the armor, my friend, and this alone that renders us invincible. These are the tactics we should study. If we lose these, we are conquered, fallen indeed...so long as our manners and principles remain sound, there is no danger."

Robert Winthrop, Speaker of the House of Representatives and mentor of Daniel Webster: "All societies must be governed in some way or other. The less they may have of stringent state government, the more they must have of individual self-government. The less they rely on public law or physical force, the more they must rely on private moral restraint. People, in the world, must necessarily be controlled, either by a power within them or by a power without them; either by the word of God or by the strong arm of man; either by the Bible or by the bayonet. It may do for other countries and other governments to talk about the state supporting religion. Here, under our free institutions, it is religion which must support the state."

During the same turbulent years of the American Revolution there was a similar discontent of the political status quo across the Atlantic but with a drastically different vision and goal. It did not mirror the free power of the people to choose their representatives and surely it was not the religious revival that took place in America before the Revolutionary War. It was the anti-religious, sexual and political French Revolution. The Age of Reason, known commonly as the Enlightenment Era, erupted with rage and revenge.

The secular revolution was branded and marketed as an anti-religious reformation. One encyclopedia article communicates this fact. The French Revolution, in particular, represented the Enlightenment philosophy through a violent and Messianic lens...The desire for rationality in government led to the attempt to end the Roman Catholic Church and indeed, Christianity in France.[5]

Leading and distinguished thinkers such as Voltaire and Rousseau challenged and influenced their French peers to reject God, the Church and the Monarchy. Deists, atheists and more united to replace religion with reason — revealed knowledge with attained knowledge. Aggressive atheism was in its infant form. Voltaire and Rousseau were radicalized years before through the writings of Baron Paul d'Holbach, who authored the first uncompromising atheist book since antiquity.[6] Rousseau, the poster child for absentee fathers, had five illegitimate children and left each one unnamed at a state-run orphanage. He did not view his abandoned children as a moral failure but as a moral achievement in the betterment of a new French society. He literally believed individuals should be owned by the government. His ideal world is when the Secular State "possess men and all their powers." [7]

As Larry Taunton explains, "Your view of God will determine your view of man, which will determine your view of government." [8] An atheist view of God will predispose someone to a statist view of government. For example, the 20th century despot, Pol Pot, studied the works of

Rousseau in Paris during the 1950s before his murderous campaign forced Cambodia back in the Iron Age.[9]

Voltaire, on the other hand, had a more controversial flare for his disdain of Christianity. Known for blunt and abhorrent remarks as "Christianity is the most ridiculous, the most absurd and bloody religion that has ever infected the world," and "every sensible man, every honest man, must hold the Christian sect in horror," then finally, "the truth of religion is never so well understood as by those who have lost the power of reasoning."

Author Stephen Kreis, of *The History Guide,* summarizes the Enlightenment figures as such: "In the final analysis, the philosophies differed widely. To speak of them as a movement is to label them a school of thought. However, what united them all was their common experience of shedding their inherited Christian beliefs with the aid of classical thinkers, specifically Roman, and for the sake of modern philosophy. They corporately agreed that Christianity was a supernatural religion. It was wrong. It was unreasonable. '"Wipe it out! Wipe out the infamous!"' shouted Voltaire. Only science, with its predictable results, was the way to truth, moral improvement and happiness." [10]

Rousseau's love for big government and Voltaire's animosity towards Christianity induced a riotous undercurrent in the people. According to famed historians, Otto Scott and Dr. Peter Hammond, this was the mood and current cultural environment on July 13, 1789, the day before the storming of the Bastille and the beginning of the bloody massacres and public hangings that would follow.

A contemporary comparison of late 18th Century France to contemporary American society.
Author's parenthetical added

- **The French movement was extremely anti-God, political groups separated themselves into the left and right. Those choosing to go against the Church, decided on their own accord, to sit on the left to mock Matthew 25** (The radical far left in American politics promotes secularism and limits religious freedom)

- **The French people cried "we want change"** (Contemporary political slogans)

- **Intellectuals were ashamed of their country** (Major universities teach a revisionist, historic picture of America to question patriotism and their love for all things global)

- **French theater promoted liberal propaganda** (Hollywood)

- **Nobles did not want lower taxes and free market** (Prefer government play a larger role*)*

- **News/Press admired agitators but never covered Church unless scandals.** (Religious revivals and local, national, global social justice ministries and projects are not highlighted by the media, only negative stories covering lawsuits and infidelity)

- **Huge debt** *(Past 17 trillion and heading towards 20 trillion)*

- **Porn circulated publicly in French Society** (Billion dollar industry in America, current Department of Justice neglects their responsibility to enforce Federal graphic pornography laws)

- **Homosexuals held public balls as police guarded carriages** (Gay pride parades)
  ***First national sodomy laws ever to be repealed happened in France following the Revolution.

- **Cults, black magic became popular** (Vampire and wizard books and movies marketed to preteens and adolescents)

- **Humanism of Voltaire and Rousseau paved the way** [11]

The similarities of angst in French society to modern America is not extraordinary, but expected. Secular humanism rooted in an atheist or deistic view of God was brought to the mainstream. The answer was bigger government for the people.

The problem was old, irrational, religious morals and restraints. Less God and increased government was the revolutionary remedy.

This blend of opposing worldviews which are incompatible with a biblical worldview would now gain further traction around the globe in the proceeding 19th and 20th centuries by influencing more known 'world changers.'

Humanism

Basic Assumption — Man is the center of all things. Man is basically good. Man is influenced by his genetics and environment, not a sinful nature. God may or may not exist but He is not involved in this world. Man must "save himself." Moral absolutes do not exist. Man decides what is good and what is evil.

World Changer: John Dewey — signed the original Humanist Manifesto in 1933. Founded the American Civil Liberties Union (ACLU) in partnership with our previous atheist lawyer Clarence Darrow and others. Founded the National Education Association (NEA), the public school teacher union and largest union in America. Additionally, he was author of the book *Common Faith,* where he described his contempt of Christianity, moral absolutes, his rejection of original sin, and man's naturally born sinful nature. He is known as the father of modern education. "The great task of the school is to counteract and transform those domestic and neighborhood tendencies...the influence of home and church." [12]

Naturalism

Basic Assumption — God does not exist. The physical, material world is all there is. Free will to make moral choices does not exist. Man is predetermined by his genetics and environment through the evolutionary process. Moral absolutes do not exist. Man decides what is good and what is evil. Man evolved from goo and has no intrinsic value.

World Changer: Charles Darwin — though not an atheist, the theory of natural selection through evolution in his book *Origin of Species* revolutionized the world, not only the scientific community. "Darwin's Dangerous Idea," labeled by his adamant supporters, led the aggressive, anti-religious ideas to engage in a full-blown culture war on faith and the existence of God. Furthermore, evolution transcends science as it integrates the naturalistic worldview into morality, philosophy, economics, and public policy.

Statism

Basic Assumption — Government is superior to the individual. Moral absolutes do not exist. Man must decide through government. Man is basically good, there is no sin. Man is influenced by his environment.

The government must change and improve the environment (society) for man to progressively evolve.

World Changer: Karl Marx — Author of the *Communist Manifesto*. Influenced the reign of terror in the twentieth century, ranging from the oppressive regimes of the Soviet Union, China and Vietnam to Nazi Germany. Marx radically applied Darwin's evolutionary ideas to economics and sociology. "The philosophers have only interpreted the world...the point however is to change the world." "The abolition of religion as the illusory happiness of the people is required for their real happiness." "We must destroy the family, we must replace home education with social." [13]

Nihilism

Basic Assumption — Nothing matters. There is no god. There is no truth. Who cares! Why try... It is all meaningless.

World Changer: Friedrich Nietzsche, a German philosopher and cultural critic. His famed assertion 'God is dead' radicalized atheistic thought to the point that life was meaningless. He preferred life had meaning but blamed Christianity for devaluing human life with the hope of an afterlife. Religion, he believed, made this life not worth living.

I hope you have been able to see the links and interconnecting points of opposing worldviews, as well as the corresponding unrest that radical,

> The problem was old, irrational, religious morals and restraints. Less God and increased government was the revolutionary remedy.

progressive ideas have on societies which have long been established on the structure of institutions, authorities and absolute morality. The French Revolution and last century's communist revolutions are prime examples. Both were anti-Christianity and pro-government.

The assumption that there is no god by the naturalists leads man to replace God's authority and sovereignty. Humanism becomes man's lofty way of dealing with God's authority. Now man is the center of this world and he must make his own morality. Statism becomes man's totalitarian way of dealing with God's sovereignty. We can manage every crisis with secular means and administrations. There is no need for God.

Drawing from Darwin's Naturalism, man is a material animal influenced by his environment. Drawing from Marx's statism, if you change the man's social and economical environment, you will thus change the man — who is influenced by his environment. Drawing from Dewey's Humanism, 'there is no need for a deity, man can save himself' through government (Humanist Manifesto II, 1973). Drawing from all three combined, man is a predetermined animal through genetics and environment which is reliant upon government to provide and progressively usher man into a global paradise. *So why try?* says the Nihilist. Legalized marijuana, food stamps, sexual irresponsibility and experimentation; it does not matter. I was born this way (genetics/naturalism) and I am unable to change (environment/statism). There is no God. There is no truth. There is no judgement. There is no sin.

All of these opposing worldviews fall under the political and philosophical banner of Progressivism. To say man is progressing or evolving socially and economically through the wise and benevolent shepherding of government to an earthly paradise, absent of God, religion, morality and judgement, is to agree with Rousseau's big government & Marx's Communism, dancing in step with Darwin's Naturalism, while holding hands with Voltaire's & Dewey's irreligious Humanism.

To quote respected theologian and highly sought after speaker, N.T. Wright, "The line of thought that has emerged from the Western world is what I refer to as the doctrine of progress. Expounded loftily by Hegel [German atheist philosopher who influenced Karl Marx] it suggested more or less that the world was progressing by means of the dialectical process. Everything was moving toward a better, fuller, more perfect end. If there had to be suffering on the way, if there had to be problems as a dialectic unwound, so be it; such things are the broken eggs from which delicious omelets are being made. The combination of technological advancement, medical advancements, progressive idealism, and social Darwinism created a climate of thought in which to this day a great many people have lived and moved." [14]

Imagine the 120 million murdered and more tortured under the oppression of twentieth century Socialism/Communism regimes as the 'broken eggs' of progress. From the social engineering of the Nazi's holocaust to the economic evolution of Stalin's Russia and Mao's China; these are the massive and oppressive omelets conjured with 'broken eggs.' That is the sum total of worldviews: when (Naturalism) persuades man to save himself (Humanism) through government intervention (statism). I prefer toast over broken eggs!

N.T. Wright again writes, "The progressivist [Humanist] thinks that things are getting better through various kinds of evolution. World War I was justified on this principle. If what matters is the survival of the fittest (Naturalism), then what we need is a good war (statism) to sort out who is best fitted to survive." [15]

Conservative columnist, Charles Krauthammer, writes "Liberalism's perfectionist ambitions — reflected in its progenitor (and current euphemism) progressivism — seeks to harness the power of government, the mystique of science and the rule of experts to shape both society and citizen and bring them both, willing or not, to a higher state of being." [16] The power of the state, under the sovereignty of self-labeled science, will force social engineering of a new morality to bring man into the next utopian society, where humanity finds its inner Messiahship and collectively 'saves themselves' without God's grace or existence.

In fairness, the progressive movement in America has done a marvelous job and should be commended for its tireless work in racial and gender equality, as well as fair wages and labor protection laws. Though socially contributing a cultural advancement to our social and economic environment, they spiritually launched a culture war. The French Revolution of yuppie and hippie college radicals turned the universities of America in the 1960s into ground zero. The trend of biblical unbelief had begun!

George Barna links today's struggles with yesterday's radical ideas. "With the social upheaval that was ushered in during the sixties, everything was up for grabs — including the national sense of morality, spirituality, values, traditions and lifestyle habits. To this day we are still experimenting and tinkering with our worldview: it remains a work in progress. The bottom line is this: the substitution of alternative worldviews for the traditional Judeo-Christian version is responsible for America's incrementally destroying itself." [17]

The post-World War II Generation, the sons and daughters of the greatest generation, are the well documented Baby Boomers. The term comes from the massive population growth and expansion of America into white picket fence suburbs and neighborhood housing developments following the war. Parents spoiled their children in an attempt to prevent them from experiencing the suffering they themselves endured during the Great Depression and World War II. Their children, eventually, ran wild in sexual liberation and an anti-traditional movement.

Forty years later, these cultural warriors, some militant and some moderate, are the behind the scene icons which run the media, government, entertainment industry and public education from elementary to the university level. According to the *Seven Faith Tribes* by George Barna, 90% of an individual's belief system is formed from the messaging and information which are propagated through these above institutions. Church holds a less serious 10% influence.

The trend of biblical unbelief which started in the 1960s has now reached epidemic proportions. A biblical worldview has been challenged by Voltaire and Dewey's Humanism, Darwin's *Dangerous Idea* of Naturalism and Rousseau and Marx's big government. This is no theory or conspiracy. Their written core beliefs want to supersede our time-honored theological beliefs.

Immediately following the upheaval of the 1960s university protests against Church and State, the progressive movement galvanized support, not only to fundamentally change the social landscape of injustice and prejudice, but to radically remake America and the world at a more intimate spiritual level. If the Enlightenment of the French was the Age of Reason, the Progressivism of the West and in particular the American youth, was the Age of Aquarius. An ultramodern world was coming; one united in religion, science, economic trade and military cooperation. The gods of this world were intentionally going higher without God in this world. The oppressiveness of religion was finally vanquished by legitimate lasciviousness, all condoned by progressive moralist governments. Clearly, the hinge of history has turned, the tipping point has moved, a coalesced world void of the rule of God is highly preferred by most, and all this deception manipulated by anti-Christian propaganda and rhetoric.

The aggressive atheists of Chapter 2 have the same end goal in mind. Their objection to God is not scientific but political. Vox Dey explicitly uncovers the agenda of the new atheists in his book *The Irrational Atheist*. "It is not the end of faith that is the ultimate goal, this is merely a necessary prerequisite to the economic cultural and moral integration required for establishing the world government that the devotees of Reason hope will bring a permanent end to war." [18] According to his research, famed atheists such as Bertrand Russell and Sam Harris blame the Christian religion for slowing global moral progress while preventing a fully reasonable and nondenominational spirituality from ever emerging in our world.

Envision such a pristine and pleasant new global village. You can if you try. The writers of the Humanist Manifesto II compiled their humanistic, atheistic, statist utopia in 1973. Shortly after the song, 'used almost equally with national anthems' around the world, per former President Jimmy Carter was composed in 1971—John Lennon's *Imagine*.[19] It is the spiritual hymn of the secular progressive movement; even rehearsed yearly in Times Square on New Year's Eve. Notice how the Humanist Manifesto and the world's anthem is almost identical.

IMAGINE lyrics — A world with no hell below us...
(rejection of judgment and accountability)

HUMANIST MANIFESTO II religion — immortal salvation or fear of eternal damnation are both illusory and harmful. They distract humans from present concerns, from self-actualization... We can discover no divine purpose or providence for the human species. While there is much that we do not know, humans are responsible for what we are or will become. No deity will save us; we must save ourselves.
(denies eternity and judgment)

IMAGINE lyrics — imagine there's no heaven...only the sky above us
(no God, denies the existence of God)

HUMANIST MANIFESTO II religion — We find insufficient evidence for belief in the existence of a supernatural; it is either meaningless or irrelevant to the question of survival and fulfillment of the human race. As non-theists, we begin with humans not God, nature not deity.
(denies God's existence)

IMAGINE lyrics — the people living for today
(here and now, no eternity, all you see is all you get)

HUMANIST MANIFESTO II ethics — Happiness and the creative realization of human needs and desires, individually and in shared enjoyment, are continuous themes of Humanism. We strive for the good life, here and now.

(literally the here and now, no eternity, all you see is all you get)

IMAGINE lyrics — imagine there is no countries and no religion too (One World Government — a united world without God)

HUMANIST MANIFESTO II world community — We deplore the division of humankind on nationalistic grounds....We thus reaffirm a commitment to the building of world community.

(The One World Government — a united world without God)

Please do not interpret this as condemning a song or artist in the name of Christ. Rather, I am informing us of the spirit of the progressive radical movement of yesteryear. This same spirit has morphed into its present position of influence; the matured business leaders of today's culture. They protested for the "one world concept" as teens coming of age. Over the past 40 years they've pursued this idea by challenging the biblical worldview which stands in contrast to their beloved humanistic view.

There is one immoveable and irresistible force that has prevented them from fulfilling their prophetic dream of a united, one world government without God, religion, or morality. A humanist, atheist, and statist fantasy of unlimited government with unchecked morality cannot progress without a struggle because of the sovereign independent superpower built on the foundation of religion and morality, America!

Gleaning back again to our founding fathers' statements earlier in this chapter, they truly believed and were convinced that our freedom and democracy could not last beyond our willingness and ability to live religious and moral lives. The game plan is not complex. Humble and crumble America by removing it from its biblical foundation of religion and morality.

Big government and free religion never blend well. Government is as a heavy, dark pollutant oil. The Church is as the crystal clear, pure water. The two do not mix. Abolish their biblical belief and introduce them to humanistic beliefs and God is no longer the center of the world;

no longer the giver of rights and protections. Man becomes the center of the world and the state decides on your rights and protections.

The Declaration of Independence holds a biblical worldview. God exists and He is involved in our lives, even granting us certain rights. "We hold these truths to be self-evident, that all men are created equal, that they are endowed by their Creator with certain unalienable Rights, that among these are Life, Liberty and the pursuit of Happiness."

Our founding fathers and modern Presidents, who were not part of the 1960s liberal reformist movement, echo this spirit. In his 1961 inaugural address, President John F. Kennedy said, "The rights of man come not from the generosity of the state but from the hand of God." Feb 15, 1959, at an Attorney General Conference, President Harry Truman warned, "If we don't have a proper fundamental moral background, we will finally end up with a totalitarian government, which does not believe in rights for anybody except the state!"

If you deny the existence of God and destroy the foundations of religion and morality our country was established upon, then Rousseau and Marx's big government will save Voltaire and Dewey's anti-religious man. The unicorns and rainbows of the new bliss, predicted by Marx using Darwin's evolutionary ideas, will at last be our new reality.

Ancient Israel grieved God as He suffered rejection from His chosen nation. His archaic methodology of 'trusting in providence' was old-school and seemed awkward to the pluralistic nations which surrounded them. Israel wanted their King to become their 'god.' Their success as a nation would not be ascribed to the God of their forefathers. Government would 'go before them' into battle.

The scriptures identify God as the One who would go before Israel.

And the Lord went before them by day in a pillar of cloud to
lead the way, and by night in a pillar of fire to give them light, so
as to go by day and night.
Exodus 13:21

For you shall not go out with haste,
Nor go by flight;
For the Lord will go before you,
And the God of Israel will be your rear guard.
Isaiah 52:12

In the days of Samuel, there was a progressive spirit in the air, a demand for more government and less religion. The people had this nasty habit of 'doing right in their own eyes.' Of course, nothing prospered while practicing an early form of Humanism. Along comes Marxism with his statist philosophies to have a King 'go before us' and become our God. Then Israel and her humanist friends can save themselves!

> But when they said, "Give us a king to lead us," this displeased
> Samuel; so he prayed to the Lord. And the Lord told him:
> "all that the people are saying to you; it is not you they have
> rejected, but they have rejected me as their king."
> **1 Samuel 8: 6-7**

> "We want a king over us. Then we will be like all the
> other nations, with a king to lead us and to
> 'go out before us' and fight our battles."
> **1 Samuel 8:19-20**

In the days of Shawn Hyland, there is, once again, a progressive spirit in the air. A comparable high demand for more government and less religion. All truth has been labeled as relative, as humanity does that which is 'right in their own eyes.' Religion and God is becoming obsolete, as reason and government is favored for our future. Moral truth and its corresponding biblical worldview belong in a bygone era. America, the bedrock of Western Christianity, known for its revivals and missionary work, might become the burial place of Western Christianity. The secularist was keenly aware of the virtuous strength which upheld our democracy. It was our acceptance and practice of the Christian faith. If by chance, America would deny the faith it would become corrupt and topple. The objective of the humanist, naturalist, and statist worldview is the establishment and erecting of an integrated world without God, religion or morality. The parasitical idea of personal and corporate redemption — sexual liberation individually and socialist economies collectively. The end goal? A secular world community without moral absolutes.

Such high aspirations demand an enormous amount of ambition and drive. What did their expertise target? Our 5 Core Beliefs. Why?

Destroy the biblical worldview and eliminate the religion of the people, thereupon eliminating the morality of that religion, thereupon eliminating the very democracy built by such religion and morality by Providence Himself. This done and you will achieve the eventual and ultimate end — to persuade a passive and uninformed populace to replace God with government in a new united, secular world without God, religion or morality. Imagine!

Be cautious not to dismiss the obvious and deny the objective data. A 2014 Reason Foundation survey shows that the Millennial Generation prefers a larger government that does not promote traditional Christian values. This is the same generation with a 1% biblical worldview. [20]

As a whole, America has not understood the relational ties between individual, moral laws which have been unscrupulously changed and the continual erosion of our privacy and rights of freedom. The redefinition of marriage, the

Destroy the biblical worldview and eliminate the religion of the people, thereupon eliminating the morality of that religion, thereupon eliminating the very democracy built by such religion and morality by Providence Himself. This done and you will achieve the eventual and ultimate end

legality of recreational drugs and the refusal to enforce pornography laws share equal airtime on the evening news as the secret programs of the NSA, the abuse of the IRS, the number of executive orders and the use of drones. Francis Schaffer often said that we see things in "bits and pieces." Nancy Pearcey writes, "We worry about things like family breakdown, violence in our schools, immoral entertainment, abortion and bioethics — a wide array of individual issues. But we don't see the big picture that connects all the dots." [21] The ambient Christian shrugs his shoulders and carelessly remarks 'it is just the way the world is today.' But the facts contradict the naivety; it isn't the way *the world is*, it's the way *the world is being made!*

I hope to change our inability to recognize and acknowledge the grand scope of our current world, its future structure, and how that correlates to biblical truth and the genuine Christ-follower. Throughout this book you will regularly notice a pattern of action and conflict by the secular movers and shakers against the principles of truth and freedom. How you respond to moral and spiritual truth, as revealed in the Scriptures, will determine your level of freedom, both politically and spiritually.

"Then you will know the truth, and the truth will set you free."
John 8:32

In Section II, we will individually consider each of these core beliefs. By using Scripture and apologetics, each belief will be proven reasonable, reliable and right! After gaining confidence in our common faith, we will discover how these beliefs give us a unique perspective on the world through a biblical lens. Though the humanist, atheist, statist and others find familiar points of agreement, they differ vastly on other points. UnDivided's 5 Core Beliefs can serve as a rallying point at which all Christianity can come into agreement. These essential and unifying basic Christian beliefs are denied by opposing worldviews and have been replaced with false assumptions and theories.

1. Deny the existence of God — replaced by unguided evolution (Creation)
2. Deny eternity and judgement — live for the here and now (Creation)
3. Deny absolute truth — all morality is relative (Bible)
4. Deny evil and sin — attribute man's actions to genetics and environment (Devil and Saved by Grace)
5. Deny the deity of Jesus Christ — replace God with government (Jesus)

To more clearly communicate how these contrasting views are in opposition to the biblical view, we need to understand the three parts of a complete worldview — Creation (origins), The Fall (cause of suffering), Redemption (how to fix the world). The following chart is a simple way to help you navigate the mutual exclusivity of these adversarial worldviews.

OPPOSING WORLD VIEWS	BIBLICAL WORLD VIEW
Origins Evolution = man is purely made of matter	**Origins** Creation = man is made in the image of God
Suffering The rise of Religion and Morality = moral restraints imposed by religious beliefs are contrary to nature's genetic desires, causing this evolved animal (Mankind) to enact evil due to his inner unrest. Newly evolved human communities invented moral laws to protect their personal possessions for mutual survival (Do Not Steal, Do Not Murder, Do Not Covet). To enforce these regulations, an unseen god was invented who judged and punished those who violated the moral laws.	**Suffering** The loss of Religion and Morality = when Mankind sinned through Adam by not trusting in God's word (loss of religion) and instead chose to make his own morality (become as gods), the curse of sin entered the world, causing natural evil (earthquakes, hurricanes, diseases, famine) and moral evil (murder, rape, theft, violence)
Redemption Remove religion and morality, and replace with a secular world government.	**Redemption** Restore religion (trust in Jesus Christ) and morality (follow Jesus Christ). Jesus will make all things new, destroying evil at His second coming, as the government rests upon His shoulder's as King of Kings and Lord of Lords.

Section 2

The Core Belief

Chapter Four

God is the Creator and is sovereign over His creation

Revealed Knowledge

In the beginning God created the heavens and the earth.
Now the earth was formless and empty, darkness was
over the surface of the deep, and the Spirit of God
was hovering over the waters.
Genesis 1:1

Then God said, "Let us make man in our image, in our likeness,
and let them rule over the fish of the sea and the birds of
the air, over the livestock, over all the earth, and over all the
creatures that move along the ground." So God created man in
his own image, in the image of God he created him;
male and female he created them.
Genesis 1:26-27

When I consider your heavens, the work of your fingers, the
moon and the stars, which you have set in place, what is man
that you are mindful of him, the son of man that you care for
him? You made him a little lower than the heavenly beings and
crowned him with glory and honor. You made him ruler over
the works of your hands; you put everything under his feet: all
flocks and herds, and the beasts of the field, the birds of the air,
and the fish of the sea, all that swim the paths of the seas.
Psalm 8:3-9

So was fulfilled what was spoken through the prophet:
"I will open my mouth in parables, I will utter things hidden
since the creation of the world."
Matthew 13:35

"Then the King will say to those on his right, 'Come, you who
are blessed by my Father; take your inheritance, the kingdom
prepared for you since the creation of the world.'"
Matthew 25:34

"But at the beginning of creation God
'made them male and female.'"
Mark 10:6

He said to them, "Go into all the world and
preach the good news to all creation."
Mark 16:15

In the beginning was the Word, and the Word was with God,
and the Word was God. He was with God in the beginning.
Through him all things were made;
without him nothing was made that has been made.
John 1:1-3

For in him all things were created: things in heaven and on
earth, visible and invisible, whether thrones or powers or rulers
or authorities; all things have been created through him and for
him. He is before all things, and in him all things hold together.
Colossians 1:16-17

Reasons to Know

The controversy of God's involvement in creation is beyond belief, no pun intended. Recently, there was a media fire storm when Answers In Genesis founder, Dr. Ken Ham debated children's scientific guru, Bill Nye the Science Guy, at the Creation Museum in Petersburg, KY on February 4, 2014. The intellectual extravaganza drew the attention of the faithful and the faith-not-full. There has never been a modern debate among scholars or experts which generated the kind of atmosphere that took place that night. It was a diluted form of UFC/WWE hype. I for one, out of the three million viewers, was in the corner for Dr. Ken Ham. This clash of origins stemmed from a Youtube video posted by Bill Nye titled, "Bill Nye: Creationism Is Not Appropriate For Children." [1] Such a title causes flashbacks to previously noted, Richard Dawkins and his comment, that teaching children religion is child abuse.

Bill Nye's video has been viewed by nearly 6.4 million people as of April 2014. In his remarks, he unfairly appropriates someone's belief in origins to their ability to design an invention, such as an engineer. If a person believes this magnificent universe is designed, is he then unqualified to design mechanical and electrical objects? Interesting Bill, interesting. In the worldview of Bill Nye, our existence is an accident. No intelligence was necessary to construct our astronomical astrophysical universe. You must believe, I stress believe not know, in an unexplainable disorder of preexisting elements by which chance, through a chaotic random explosion, resulted in a completely opposite principled, ordered and scientifically observable universe with laws, physics and intricate fine-tuning points to sustain life. Mr. Nye is convinced that it takes intelligent planning to lay a foundation and erect a tower as an engineer or architect, but the plural universes suspended in a realm of time; no thought required. His early frustration in this video towards those who refuse to assume origins as he interprets them, slowly transitions into a hopeful glee as he states, "In another couple centuries, that world view [creationism] I am sure, won't exist."

I give him props for saying that evolution and creationism is a world view. As we know, a worldview is based on assumption and goes beyond the limited realm of science as it flaunts its influence into laws, family values, politics and man's nature. The world view of Naturalism, so associated with science and evolution is not only based on assumptions but built on unanswered questions such as: where did water come from? What is in the core of the earth? How did the moon get here? Where did life come from? Where did oxygen come from? [2]

Scientists who adamantly cling to evolution as the answer to our current existence fail miserably to address the origin of the universe and the origin of life. How we got here does not address why we got here. If your long lost relative was to knock on your door and you were to inquisitively ask, "why are you here?" and they responded, "I left at 9:30am, took the highway to exit 80, stopped for lunch, took the backroad to avoid traffic, made a left at the light and stayed straight till I got here," you would politely interrupt and restate your original inquiry. Not 'how' did you get here, but why are you here? What is the reason? What is your purpose? That would be your fair response. The theory of evolution focuses on the 'how did we get here,' not the 'why are we here origin.' It illustrates a long billion year journey through deep space and time. It does not answer how time or the matter and energy that fills space came into being. Honestly, it does not empirically prove 'how' we arrived at our destination or stage of development. Evolutionists attempt to give credibility to their theory by using 'time' to explain the unexplainable. Creationists attempt to give credibility to their theory by using 'God' to explain the unexplainable.

I will not venture to prove the various theories of intelligent design, creationism, young universe, old universe, gap theory or the host of other interpretations and propositions. However, using the scientific law of cause and effect, what is the most likely beginning (cause) of the universe (effect)? I am confident that we can conclude there is a God and that we are made through His power, His intelligence and by His will. To a much higher degree, biblically, we are made in His image.

Science is not sovereign. It is not all powerful. It is not all knowing. What is science? The Oxford English Dictionary answers that question, "the intellectual and practical activity encompassing the systematic study of the structure and behavior of the physical and natural world through observation and experiment." As Vox Dey persuasively points out,

> "Science is the systematic study done through observation and experiment. Therefore, if the study is not systematic, or if observation and experiment are not involved, it is obviously not science by this definition." [3]

God, by the very definition, is unobservable and cannot be experimented upon. God is beyond science. God is everywhere. You cannot hide from His presence. He is separate, different and independent from His creation. He is the holy, all knowing, all powerful, eternal, unchanging, perfect, triune, good, loving, merciful, gracious, compassionate, patient, truthful, faithful and just God.

Science observes the current state of the universe ranging from the gases in galaxies to the biology of DNA that is our genetic family tree. The Bible does not contradict observable science. Science can explain the matter and energy which is in the universe but it cannot explain where these elements came from. 'In the beginning' is a major stumbling block, not because of observation but because of assumption.

> "Science is the systematic study done through observation and experiment. Therefore, if the study is not systematic, or if observation and experiment are not involved, it is obviously not science by this definition." [3]

Let us discover the implications of Genesis to our existence compared to a nonmaterial beginning. First, science has proven that matter and energy, the building blocks of our universe, are not eternal. The universe is not everlasting. It had a beginning and it will run its course and have its end. Please do not equate the Sci-Fi, B-movie to understand the picture described in these words. Something cannot come from nothing. Consequently, everything that exists has to be temporal, with a beginning or eternal, without a beginning.

All present-day cosmology theories lead to a universe with a beginning point.

Many scientists support theories on the expansion of the universe and the evolution of our biological world.

All theories are based on the Big Bang 'in the beginning,' explosive starting point! Science and religion singing the glory of God in perfect harmony. Dinesh D'Souza communicates the harmony, "In a stunning confirmation of the book of Genesis, modern scientists have discovered that the universe was created in a primordial explosion of energy and light...Space and time did not exist prior to the universe. If you accept that everything that has a beginning has a cause, then the material universe had a nonmaterial or spiritual cause." [4]

Observation is a method to eliminate competing theories. Observing the effects does not automatically make known the cause. Picture the driveway of your house being wet. The wetness can be observed by sight and touch. However, proving through observation the wetness of your concrete matter does not automatically explain how the concrete became wet. The competing theories could possibly include: it rained, the sprinklers went on, someone washed their car, someone spilled their drink, someone watered the grass, or more. Science has observed the effects of the Big Bang as the water in the driveway; the radiation background and the expansion of the universe

> All present-day cosmology theories lead to a universe with a beginning point.

from the starting point of, well...creation. The Big Bang theory lends itself to a theistic view of an eternal God outside of space and time, creating or causing the material universe of space and time. This is the best, plausible cause for the universe.

The Second Law of Thermodynamics states that over time the universe is breaking down. Physical life dies and non-life decays. Scientists' understanding of the universe was inaccurate for many years until the Hubble Telescope changed the mind of Albert Einstein and the scientific community. The universe was not stagnant and eternal. Planets and entire galaxies were careening away from one another. The universe was massive and moving outward. It was the perpetual effects of a dynamic explosion that, at its humble beginnings, was smaller than a single atom. Jesus said the Kingdom of God is like a seed. Equally, the universe is like an atom. 'Let there be light' is the word that brought the worlds into existence. The word is continually causing this unstoppable explosion.

> By faith we understand that the worlds were framed by the word of God, so that the things which are seen were not made of things which are visible.
> **Hebrews 11:3 NKJV**

Arno Penzias, who won the Nobel prize for discovering the cosmic background of radiation that corroborated the Big Bang said, "The best data we have is exactly what I would have predicted had I nothing to go on but the five books of Moses, the Psalms, and the Bible as a whole."[5] Astronomer Robert Jastrow has been famously quoted for his humble perspective, "For the scientists who has lived by faith in the power of reason, the story ends like a bad dream. He has scaled the mountains of ignorance; he is about to conquer the highest peak. As he pulls himself over the final rock, he is greeted by a band of theologians who have been sitting there for centuries." [6]

Ken Ham is resolute and unwavering in his stand for Genesis creationism. "The Genesis compromise has been highly destructive to the church in regard to biblical authority. It has greatly contributed to the decline of the church in America, including the exodus of so many young people from the church." [7] Too often, the Church distances themselves from the creation account of Genesis to avoid seeming unsophisticated. Moses could have started the Bible with 'in the beginning, man was in the garden,' but the Holy Spirit did not inspire him to do so. Neither should the Church be ashamed of the Genesis narrative as if it asserted a fable or Greek style mythology account. Genesis 1:3 'let there be light,' was the big bang of explosive energy. Genesis 1:4, the separation of light and day is the formation of the sun and moon.

Now to the more divisive and controversial theory of evolution, which biologically, is vastly different from the Big Bang theory of matter and energy combusting to form space and time. The origin of life is distinct from the origin of the universe even though both are impossible without God.

Evolution, as described by Charles Darwin, is based on the 'change of kinds.' In hindsight, he was too optimistic as he predicted 150 years ago that scientists would unearth numerous transitional fossils to produce evidence of his hypothesis. As of today, not one transitional fossil has ever turned up.

Dr. Colin Patterson, an evolutionist with the British Museum of Natural History, said concerning a book he wrote that did not include a single picture of a transitional fossil, "I fully agree with your comments on the lack of direct illustration of evolutionary transitions in my book. If I knew of any, fossil or living, I would have certainly have included them. You suggest an artist should be used to visualize such transformations but where would he get the information from? I could not honestly provide it and if I were to leave it to artistic license would that not mislead the reader? I am much occupied with the philosophical problems of identifying ancestral forms in the fossil record. You say that I should at least show a photo of the fossil from which each type of organism was derived. I will lay it on the line — there is not one such fossil for which one could make a watertight argument." [8]

Evolution itself would be a true metaphysical miracle.

The New Oxford American Dictionary defines a miracle as "a surprising event that is not explicable by natural or scientific laws and is therefore considered to be the work of a divine agency." Brannon Howse compares the miraculous transitional fossils, that they are unable to find, against known scientific laws. "Naturalistic evolutionists would have us believe everything happened by random spontaneity — life chanced to come about from non-life; matter came into existence from nothing." [9]

To clarify, an evolutionist must believe that living things came mysteriously from nonliving things as matter and energy. Again, intelligent life came strangely through non-intelligent matter. At what point did dead matter transform into living cells? Remember, their answer cannot be a barely plausible theory. It must be observable and experimental. The origin of evolutionary life is neither. Dr. Robert A. Millikan, a physicist and Nobel prize winner, stated in a speech before the American Chemical Society "the pathetic thing about it is that many scientists are trying to prove the doctrine of evolution, which no science can do." [10] He is not the only scientist that is frustrated by dogmatic, authoritative propaganda that evolution is a fact. Dr. D. M. S. Watson, Professor of Zoology and Comparative Anatomy at University College, London, writes: "Evolution . . . is accepted by zoologists not because it has been observed to occur or . . . can be proved by logically coherent evidence to be true, but because the only alternative, special creation, is clearly incredible." [11]

> Evolution itself would be a true metaphysical miracle.

In contrast, micro evolution is observable. This falls into line of survival and adaptation of the species. This is routinely seen in the mutations of bacteria. Macro Evolution is when one species changes into another species. This is the Darwinian 'change of kinds' that cannot be proven yet is the forced fed theory of biological evolution in our public school classrooms.

Darrow Miller, the founder of Disciple Nations Alliance, reminds us of the unproven and unexplainable gaps from non-life to life. "Two big evidence gaps confront proponents of macro-evolution. There is the gap (multiple gaps, actually) in the fossil record, and what could be called the meta-gap, i.e., the issue of how life began. A chasm exists between non-living matter and life." [12]

As stated earlier, I am not qualified to defend or persuade the various Intelligent Design and Creationist theories. Undeniably, our universe looks as if it was designed. Macro-evolution is unsubstantiated and all scientists agree that our universe had a beginning that is beyond their scope to expound upon. Richard Dawkins concedes, "No one has the [evolutionary] explanation for the origin of life...biology is the study of complicated things that give the appearance of having been designed for a purpose." [13]

Occam's Razor is a problem solving philosophy. It states that when among competing hypotheses, the one with the fewest assumptions should be selected. Anglican Clergy, Williams Paley says, "If there is a watch, then there must be a watchmaker." Nancy Pearcey, in her masterpiece book *Total Truth*, asks the reader to decide, "How can we best account for the origin of complex specified sequences of DNA — by chance, by law or by design?" [14] God as creator of the universe is a worldview assumption but it has the fewest assumptions compared to unanswered questions concerning the origin of the universe and the origin of life.

Reality Known

Man is divinely created in the image of God. Creation was a willed and purposeful act from the Godhead. Life does not come into being by sexual reproduction alone. God is sovereignly involved. The Genesis creation account is more than the account of God's intelligent handiwork. There is day and night, seedtime and harvest, male and female. Mathematical or moral anarchy will strain our peaceful and ordered existence into chaos: a day without sun, a year without rain, a civilization with misconstrued gender identities.

The Church must be unrelenting in our stand for the sanctity of life. Humanity has purpose as the sovereign Creator has a plan. President Ronald Reagan said it best, "Every legislator, every doctor, and every citizen needs to recognize that the real issue is whether to affirm and protect the sanctity of all human life, or to embrace a social ethic where some human lives are valued and others are not."

On the polar opposite of this polarizing issue are the Iowa Democrats who on August 28, 2013, gathered at their state capitol to pray that God would 'expand abortion rights' as they thanked Him for the 'blessing of choice.' [15] That is one prayer meeting that Lou Engle, from The Call, would never assemble! He prays to end abortion and send revival.

A survival of the fittest Darwinian view has penetrated our society to make life only as valuable as the collective community dictates it should be.

In December 2013, a Washington State couple received a whopping $50 million settlement because their child had a birth defect, that if properly notified by the hospital, they would have aborted. [16] There is no intrinsic value to human life or existence. If you could crush an ant you can terminate a child. This might sound radical but it is ethically reasonable according to experts.

A prime proponent of devaluing human life is the Professor of Ethics at Princeton University, Peter Singer. A man the New Yorker Magazine called "the most influential living philosopher" and Time Magazine named one of the 100 most influential men in the world.[17] Singer publicly endorses medical experimentation on the mentally disabled, denying care to the elderly and even denying rights to infants under the age of two. He believes mothers should have a trial period where they decide whether to keep their baby or not. In fact, Mr. Singer advocates the slaughter of the unborn in the womb and outside the womb up to age two, purely based on whether or not that child may be "inconvenient" or "undesirable." He has said in his book *Practical Ethics*, "Human babies are not born self aware, or capable of grasping that they exist over time. They are not persons ... animals are self aware... the life of a newborn is of less value than the life of a pig, a dog, or a chimpanzee."

The value of life is comparable to the moral code of marriage and sexuality. Each gender was created with purpose. God made the male and the female. If this simple biological and biblical principle is controversial today, what will be controversial and irreconcilable to our culture in forty years? When Jesus was asked about marriage in the context of divorce he didn't appeal to reason or Roman culture. The backbone of his moral, authoritative reply was Genesis. "In the beginning God created them male and female." Marriage is an act of

sovereign creation, not government contracts or civil rights. The government is morally limited to respect and recognize the marriage union,
not repeal marriage laws for more sexually permissive ones.

Man was created to procreate and care for his mate. Sexual reproduction was confined to the covenant of marriage. Due to the curse
of sickness and death that was introduced to this world through the sin of Adam and Eve, some-times couples are unable to conceive. However, the original creation termed

> A survival of the fittest Darwinian view has penetrated our society to make life only as valuable as the collective community dictates it should be.

'good' by God had, at its foundation, a male and a female reproducing
children in a faithful monogamous marriage relationship. Children would
need both the masculine and feminine characteristics of God that only
a father and mother combined can offer. The Genesis creation account
is more than the account of God's existence or his intelligent handiwork.

Male and female were created to work as they raised their children
and tended to the Garden of Eden. Labor is good. Production is good.
God works. God creates. We are made in His image to work, create and
prosper. The Bible clearly admonishes us:

Those who work their land will have abundant food,
but those who chase fantasies have no sense.
Proverbs 12:11

And we urge you, brothers and sisters,
warn those who are idle and disruptive, encourage the
disheartened, help the weak, be patient with everyone.
1 Thessalonians 5:14

The one who is unwilling to work shall not eat.
2 Thessalonians 3:10

According to University of Iowa professor, Benjamin Kline's book
Free Time, Americans need to work less and enjoy more time studying
and listening to music to find their higher purpose. Humanism must
be horrified that our higher purpose is to work and raise our family. It

must be no surprise that progressive, secular Europe works less than the average American. [18]

Finally, moral boundaries with corresponding responsibility and accountably was an act of creation. You can have any tree, but not that one....that is your limit...that's the boundary. That is Core Belief #2.

Chapter Five

The Bible is 100% true and its moral teachings apply today

Revealed Knowledge

Now the serpent was more crafty than any of the wild animals the LORD God had made. He said to the woman, "Did God really say, 'You must not eat from any tree in the garden'?" The woman said to the serpent, "We may eat fruit from the trees in the garden, but God did say, 'You must not eat fruit from the tree that is in the middle of the garden, and you must not touch it, or you will die." "You will not certainly die," the serpent said to the woman. "For God knows that when you eat from it your eyes will be opened, and you will be like God, knowing good and evil." When the woman saw that the fruit of the tree was good for food and pleasing to the eye, and also desirable for gaining wisdom, she took some and ate it. She also gave some to her husband, who was with her, and he ate it. Then the eyes of both of them were opened...
Genesis 3:1-7

"You shall not at all do as we are doing here today—every man doing whatever is right in his own eyes—
Deuteronomy 12:8

In those days there was no king in Israel; everyone did what was right in his own eyes.
Judges 17:6

Do not be wise in your own eyes; fear the LORD and shun evil.
Proverbs 3: 7

The fear of the LORD is the beginning of wisdom, and
knowledge of the Holy One is understanding.
Proverbs 9:10

For this cause I was born, and for this cause I have come into
the world, that I should bear witness to the truth.
Everyone who is of the truth hears My voice."
Pilate said to Him, "What is truth?
John 18:37-38

For the law was given through Moses, but grace and truth came
through Jesus Christ.
John 1:17

I am the way, the truth, and the life.
John 14:6

Sanctify them through your word, your word is truth.
John 17:17

For the time will come when they will not endure sound
doctrine, but according to their own desires, because they have
itching ears, they will heap up for themselves teachers;
and they will turn their ears away from the truth...
2 Timothy 4:3-4

For the wrath of God is revealed from heaven against all
ungodliness and unrighteousness of men,
who suppress the truth in unrighteousness.
Romans 1:18

...who exchanged the truth of God for the lie, and worshiped
and served the creature rather than the Creator...
Romans 1:25

...but to those who are self-seeking and do not obey the truth...
Romans 2:8

I make known the end from the beginning,
from ancient times, what is still to come.
Isaiah 46:10

For we did not follow cleverly devised stories when we told you
about the coming of our Lord Jesus Christ in power, but we
were eyewitnesses of his majesty.
2 Peter 1:16

Above all, you must understand that no prophecy of Scripture
came about by the prophet's own interpretation of things. For
prophecy never had its origin in the human will, but prophets,
though human, spoke from God as they were
carried along by the Holy Spirit.
2 Peter 1:20-21

...just as our dear brother Paul also wrote you with the wisdom
that God gave him. He writes the same way in all his letters,
speaking in them of these matters. His letters contain some
things that are hard to understand, which ignorant and unstable
people distort, as they do the other Scriptures,
to their own destruction.
2 Peter 3:16

Reasons to Know

Mark Burnett and Roma Downey's hit miniseries *The Bible* broke cable TV records and stirred up expected Church criticism by some and support by others. Rarely is there something as magnetic and alienating as the Holy Scriptures. Their powerfully produced thematic and cinematic story, from Genesis to Revelation, was condensed to ten hours. A hard feat to pull off yet it won three Emmy Awards and accumulated over 100 million TV views. Love it or hate it, the Bible wields influence. I doubt *The Book of Mormon* or *The Bhagavad Gita* could have followed suit.

In a *Wall Street Journal* opinion piece that was printed the day the first episode aired, Mark and Roma wrote a compelling case for the advancement of Bible knowledge in our world. "The Bible has affected the world for centuries in innumerable ways, including art, literature, philosophy, government, philanthropy, education, social justice and humanitarianism. One would think that a text of such significance would be taught regularly in schools. Not so. That is because of the "stumbling block" (the Bible again) that is posed by the powers that be in America. It's time to change that for the sake of the nation's children. It's time to encourage, perhaps even mandate, the teaching of the Bible in public schools as a primary document of Western civilization." [1]

Mark Burnett, the mastermind behind reality TV, does have a firm grasp on reality itself. The Bible has changed the world for the better and the world has opposed it in return. The written word has experienced the same fate as the living word, Jesus Christ.

> He came to that which was his own,
> but his own did not receive him.
> **John 1:11**

How does a long ago collection of various writings accumulated and canonized from an Eastern Mediterranean Civilization become the source of wisdom for Western Civilization the past 2,000 years? How can an ancient shepherd as Moses reveal the commencement of the world 2,000 years after the fact, and a common man as John the Apostle reveal the consummation of the age 2,000 years before its possible conclusion? How can all the history, narratives, prophecies and instructions weave together in perfect unison to tell the greatest story ever told? Why are entire scholarly departments dedicated to preserve and translate the text for their deep, rich meaning?

I believe it is inspired and reliable. Others rebuff it as inconsistent and contradicting. Richard Dawkins in his book *The God Delusion* says, "To be fair, much of the Bible is not systematically evil but just plain weird, as you would expect of a chaotically cobbled-together anthology of disjointed documents, composed, revised, translated, distorted and 'improved' by hundreds of anonymous authors, editors and copyists, unknown to us and mostly unknown to each other, spanning nine centuries." As you most likely presumed, I disagree.

First, let us cover the historical background. The Bible was written by approximately forty different authors in three languages, Hebrew, Aramaic and Greek, over a period of 1,600 years. This range is tallied from the timeline of the first 'written' book of Job in about 1500BC to the book of Revelation in 90AD.

Most of the Old Testament was written in Hebrew, starting from Moses' who wrote Genesis to Deuteronomy, known as the Pentateuch in 1450-1400 BC. In 586BC, Jerusalem was destroyed by the Babylonian King Nebuchadnezzar. The Jews were taken into captivity to Babylon. They remained in Babylon under the Medo-Persian Empire and there began to speak Aramaic. Therefore, the Book of Daniel chapters 2:4 to 7:28 and Ezra chapters 4:8 to 6:18; and 7:12-26 were written in Aramaic.

The New Testament was written in Greek. The Pauline Epistles and synoptic gospels of Matthew, Mark, and Luke were written between 45AD-63AD. The later Gospel of John and Revelation was written around 90-95AD.

The New Testament was canonized as the final and complete revealed Word of God under the directive of Constantine to religiously unite the Roman Empire. For the books to be officially accepted as truly inspired and equal to the Old Testament, it must have met three points of criteria. One, Apostolic Authority — written by an apostle or someone who was an eyewitness to an apostle. Second, Conformed to the Rule of Faith — i.e., Jesus was God and man, physically died on the cross and rose again. Third, Continuous Usage and Acceptance — early church fathers quoted them and the Church at large read them.

Next, let us test the authenticity of Scripture. One such method is the Bibliographic Test. In other words, how many manuscripts are available and what is the time span of those manuscripts compared to the date of the original writing. Focused strictly on the New Testament, as that is where most of the criticism is concentrated on, the time span from the original writings to partial or fragmented manuscripts is about 50 years. However, the time from the earliest writings to the first complete manuscript is only 225 years. That is exceptional compared to other ancient writings such as Aristotle and Plato, that have a time span of 1,000-1,400 years between the original and the first available complete manuscript.

Time is one measurement. The amount of manuscript copies is another. Once more, the Bible is unequaled compared to other writings of antiquity. There are 24,286 handwritten historical copies. That is an abundance of evidence. The second most verified work of antiquity is Homer's *Iliad* with 643 copies. Followed in a distant third by *Caesar's Gallic Wars* with a meager ten copies.

Time and quantity of manuscripts are vital in establishing the reliability and authenticity of the Bible. The primary question is "is what we have today the actual words of the original authors or has it been tampered and updated?" If the Apostles, who primarily penned the New Testament, wrote these stories hundreds of years after the event, then there might be historical inaccuracies that no eyewitness could correct or verify. We know this is not the case. Second, even though the Apostles were present at these events and recorded what they had firsthand experienced, did later translators and scribes alter the authentic text to add or change the meaning entirely? Again, we can be confident this is not case as the 24,000+ copies from partial, fragmented and completed manuscripts confirm the authenticity of the texts. That is to say, what we have today is what they had back then, and what they had back then is what they experienced. The Apostle Peter did exclaim, "We did not follow cleverly devised stories, but were eyewitnesses."

On the other hand, there are admittedly hundreds of thousands of variants within these manuscripts. Please keep in mind, hundreds of thousands of word variants become single digits per copy when dealing with 24,000 manuscripts in total. Keep the faith, none of these variants effect the accuracy or the meaning of the verse. 80% are categorized as spelling errors. This does not diminish the original author's divine inspiration in writing. It does show human fallibility in copying without spellcheck and fluorescent lighting. Further variants include pronouns, i.e., 'Jesus taught them' can be read in some manuscripts as 'He taught them.' Then there are some words that could not be properly translated into Latin from Greek. I stress, and scholars agree, none of these variants effect what we believe.

Additionally, there have been controversies and contentions, both within Judaism and Christianity amongst themselves, in interpreting a certain text or tradition. The Church historically has called for Council of Bishops to discuss and debate such disagreements. Normally, they would decide on a conclusion and a final authoritative Church answer to end the controversy. Never did they accept one position and then amend or update the Scriptures to support their argument. The Bible, on no account, has been updated or revised to fit church doctrine.

Beyond the Bibliographic test, is the Internal Evidence Test. Do the Scriptures contradict each other? Contradiction is too strong of a word. Different perspectives telling the same story from different angles explain most, if not all, so-called biblical contradictions. Often times, critics will try to exploit the resurrection account as a contradiction. One gospel writer gives more details than another writer, but none contradict or clash with the other. This is similar to eyewitness accounts at any live event. For instance, a police officer interviews multiple witnesses at the scene of an accident. One might offer a detail that the other left out.

Finally, there is the External Evidence Test. Are the historical events in the Bible recorded and documented in other sources of antiquity separate from the Bible or Church records? Quoting Dr. Norm Giesler, all of these facts are written by historians outside of the Bible or Church history (non-Christian sources): 1. Jesus was from Nazareth 2. He lived a wise and virtuous life 3. He was crucified in Palestine under Pontius Pilate during the reign of Tiberius Caesar at Passover time, being considered the Jewish king 4. He was believed by his disciples to have been raised from the dead three days later 5. His enemies acknowledge that he performed unusual feats they called "sorcery" 6. His small band of disciples multiplied rapidly spreading even as far as Rome 7. His disciples denied polytheism, lived moral lives and worshipped Christ as divine. [2]

Equally astounding evidence for Old Testament narratives include names of cities, people and social customs culturally relevant to the times of the historical narrative and knowledge of covenantal practices. This information has been discovered through amazing excavations in archeology from Egypt to Babylon.

A strong argument in defense of Scripture are the eyewitness accounts and their personal accountability for sharing their testimony. From the prophets to the apostles, what they saw is what they wrote, and what they wrote is what we have today, documented through available ancient manuscripts. The manuscripts prove the consistency and reliability of the Scriptures, they do not prove the accuracy of the eye witness account. However, common sense rules out the idea of lying. First, what was the benefit of outlandish and controversial lies. The apostles were murdered as martyrs for telling their story. If their story was a lie, would not at least one recant and deny the faith? None did.

The Bible has endured intense criticism since the Enlightenment. Many have tried vigorously to prove the Bible false and historically inaccurate. The Bible has proven to be unique in its ability to survive these onslaughts. Many have banned it and burned it, while others have questioned it and ridiculed it. Yet, the Bible remains authoritative, accurate, and above all, life changing. It is a historical masterpiece that has circulated around the world while being translated into 1,400 languages. But is it inspired and God-breathed, and can that be proven?

The Bible professes to be the Word of God. Critics spurn the self-proclaimed, absolute authority of the Bible by suggesting a defense that runs along the path of circular reasoning: *the Bible is infallible because the Bible is the Word of God, because the Bible claims to be the Word of God.* The most ardent of antagonistic atheists are not required to exhibit how elementary such a defense sounds. Gladly, this was not God's defense of His behind-the-scenes involvement. God separated the false religions from the true revelation by encouraging us to examine the power of prophecy.

God regularly instructed His people to recognize His inspiration of the prophets as they were able to tell 'the end from the beginning.' The Bible has thousands of prophecies, many fulfilled and much to be fulfilled. The predominant predictions consisted of the first and second coming of the Messiah, Jesus Christ and the restoration of Israel in the last of the last days.

The Apostles would quote fulfilled prophecy throughout the book of Acts to prove that Jesus was the Christ.

A sample, but not exhaustive, list of fulfilled prophecies describing His coming include:

- The Messiah Will Be Born In Bethlehem
- The Messiah Will Be Born Of A Virgin
- The Messiah Will Be A Prophet Like Moses
- The Messiah Will Be Tempted By Satan
- The Messiah Will Enter Jerusalem Triumphantly
- The Messiah Will Be Rejected By His Own People
- The Messiah Will Be Betrayed By One Of His Followers

- The Messiah Will Be Betrayed For 30 Pieces Of Silver
- The Messiah Will Be Tried And Condemned
- The Messiah Will Be Silent Before His Accusers
- The Messiah Will Be Smitten And Spat Upon
- The Messiah Will Be Mocked And Taunted
- The Messiah To Die By Crucifixion, With Pierced Hands & Feet
- The Messiah Will Suffer With Sinners
- The Messiah's Garments Will Be Divided By Casting Lots
- The Messiah's Bones Will Not Be Broken
- The Messiah Will Die As A Sin Offering
- The Messiah Will See His Seed
- The Messiah Will Be Buried In A Rich Man's Tomb
- The Messiah Will Be Raised From The Dead
- The Messiah Will Sit At God's Right Hand [3]

The restored nation of Israel is a current, supernatural phenomenon. After 2,600 years of Gentile dominance ranging from the Babylonian captivity, Roman rule and the Diaspora across the world in 70AD and 135AD, God brought His people back from the worst point in human history; The Holocaust. The Jews, knowing Europe was not a safe haven, rightfully wanted their own sovereign nation. Impossibilities never limit God's providence. On May 14, 1948, David Ben-Gurion entered the Tel Aviv Museum proclaiming "This right is the natural right of the Jewish people to be masters of their own fate like all other nations in their own sovereign state. Accordingly, we are here assembled and by virtue of our natural and historic right and on the strength of the resolution of the General Assembly of the United Nations, hereby declare the establishment of the Jewish State of Eretz-Israel, to be known as the state of Israel." [4] Ezekiel's breath (Ezekiel 36, 37) was received by this valley of dry bones. They lived and they returned!

Christian Evangelicals are not the only group that link the new nation of Israel to the ancient prophets. "I believe that if you do not know how to read the Bible, you cannot understand the daily newspaper. If you do not know the biblical story of Abraham, Isaac, and Jacob, you cannot possibly understand the miracle of the modern state of Israel." Rabbi Binyamin Elon, member of the Israeli Knesset. [5]

Jesus also quoted the Old Testament prophets and narratives to answer questions and to prove His divinity. Jesus viewed and used the Law and the Prophets as the absolute word of God.

Josh McDowell states, "We could cite many reasons for the Old Testament being God's word, but the strongest argument comes from the Lord Jesus Christ Himself. As God in human flesh, Jesus speaks with final authority. And his testimony regarding the Old Testament is loud and clear. Jesus believed that the Old Testament was divinely inspired, the veritable Word of God. He said, "The Scripture cannot be broken" (John 10:35). He referred to Scripture as "the commandment of God" (Matthew 15:3) and as the "Word of God" (Matthew 15:6). He also indicated that it was indestructible: "Until Heaven and earth pass away, not the smallest letter or stroke shall pass away from the law, until all is accomplished" (Matthew 5:18). Notice that He mentions even words and letters!"

"When dealing with the people of His day, whether it was with the disciples or religious rulers, Jesus constantly referred to the Old Testament: "Have you not read that which was spoken to you by God?" (Matthew 22:31); "Yea; and have you never read, 'Out of the mouth of infants and nursing babes thou hast prepared praise for thyself?'" (Matthew 21:16, citing Psalm 8:2); and "Have you not read what David did?" (Matthew 12:3) Examples could be multiplied to demonstrate that Jesus was conversant with the Old Testament and its content. He quoted from it often and He trusted it totally." [6]

Reality Known

Absolute truth absolutely exists. Others oppose such a statement with a puzzling response, 'absolute truth does not exist,' which by nature would be an absolute statement of truth. As Christians, we hold firm to the fact that truth does exists. Jesus Christ is the truth as He is the living word — *rhema*, identical in nature to the written word — logos. The Word is Truth.

The logical Law of Non-Contradiction states that two opposite statements cannot both be correct. Either one is correct and one is not, or they are both incorrect. Either, the Bible is absolute truth or the Bible is not absolute truth, but it cannot be true for me, yet not true for another.

There is a difference between subjective truth and objective truth. A subjective truth, known as relative truth, is a statement or belief that is personally true to you but may not necessarily apply to another. For example, 'It is hot outside.' Individuals might vary in their opinion of 'hot.' Such a statement is subjective truth. As they say, beauty is in the eye of the beholder, or he has a face that only a mother could love. Both are subjective statements of personal relative truth.

The Bible, however, falls under the definition of objective truth or absolute truth. It is God's word, as noted throughout this chapter. It is true by fact, not merely by personal feeling. For example, 'The thermometer reads a temperature of 85 degrees outside.' The personal feeling or adjective of hot, warm, or cold is subjective. The actual numeric gauge of 85 degrees is a fact or objective statement.

Jesus is Lord and Savior — subjective or objective? A person's accomplishments are a fact. The amount of accolades one receives is the opinion of the audience or judges. If I was to say, Abraham Lincoln was the 10th President, you could rightly and justly correct my unintelligible recollection of history. I cannot personally believe he was the 10th President, as another personally believes he was the 19th President. It is a fact that he was the 16th President. Facts are not open to feelings or interpretations. On the other hand, if I was to say Lincoln was the greatest President, that is a statement of personal truth.

Jesus is the Son of God, the Lord and Savior of the World, because the Bible, which we can be confident is indeed God's word, declares Him to be. This is equivalent to Lincoln being the 16th President. Using the Law of Non-Contradiction, Jesus is Lord could be wrong but it cannot be right for me yet wrong for you. It is not subjective. It is an objective statement. Absolutely right or absolutely wrong — surely not relative and up for personal interpretation.

In society, we are taught that facts must come from empirical evidence while what is good, true, right, wrong, kind, compassionate, beautiful and even religious faith are all matters of opinion. The Bible transcends philosophical limits and terms because God's word is not a matter of man's opinion. It is God's permanent and unchanging, objective moral commands, and revelation of who He is.

Moral objectivism is possible if (1) it transcends standards — can be applied to everyone and (2) man has free will — able to obey or disobey on their own decision making ability. If someone 'ought' to do something, that implies that they 'can' do it. When God says, "Thou shall not commit adultery," that implies man can make moral choices to live an adultery-free life. Thankfully, when man fails to make obedient, God-honoring, moral choices there is an offer of forgiveness as the penalty was paid by Jesus Christ!

The Humanist Manifesto II Ethics section states, "We affirm that moral values derive their source from human experience. Ethics is autonomous and situational, needing no theological or ideological sanction..." Denying the Scriptures as God's objective holy word makes it easy to abandon the belief that objective morality exists. It is no coincidence that in 1973, the year the Humanist Manifesto II was written, the moral slippery slope of America started its downward slide. Abortion became a federally legal constitutional right at a horrendous cost of 50 million unborn children. Homosexuality was relabeled by the American Psychiatric Association from a 'disorder' to normal. The sexual revolution had their Independence Day!

Note — 1973 was a progressively giant leap into our new secular global world.

The Yom Kippur War, the largest Israeli/Arab conflict occurred, the World Trade Center opened, the European Union expanded and above all, America brokered a deal with Saudi Arabia. This deal stated that all Saudi oil exported to any country must be made by the American dollar. Thus, the dollar was now backed up at the international level by oil and not the previous gold standard. This made the Middle East the central part of the world's economy.

But I digress.

Moral Relativism, put forth so well in the Human Manifesto II, believes that absolute, objective morality does not exist. There is no higher standard. There is no absolute good or absolute evil.

There are obvious problems with subjective relativism:

1. Relativism is self-defeating.
    The relativist believes that subjective truth is true for everyone, not just for them. This is the one thing they cannot believe, if they are a relativist. Therefore, if a relativist thinks it is true for everyone, then he believes it is an absolute truth. Therefore, he is no longer a relativist.

2. Relativism is full of contradictions.
    If Billy Graham believed God exists and an atheist believes God did not exist, both would be right. God would have to exist and not exist. If the Christian believes Jesus died on the Cross and the Muslim believes Jesus did not die on the Cross, both would be right. Logically and physically, this cannot be.

3. Relativism means no one has ever been wrong.
    With subjective truth, no one can ever be wrong since there is no standard for right and wrong. As long as something is true to the beholder of truth, it is true even if it is wrong for someone else.

Materialism views morality in a similar fashion. Ethics are relative, personal preferences. These 'preferences' on how to live and abide by one's own personal, moral code have been predetermined by genetics through evolution. As noted, moral objectivity is only possible when there is a higher standard and the individual moral agent can decide if they will obey. This act of decision, or power to choose, is 'free will.' Core Belief #4, will cover this in detail.

Materialists, such as atheists, reject the long held religious belief of original sin. They believe man is genetically wired to do certain acts that religion has defined as immoral. The standard of sin is unfair as no moral act is either sinful or not sinful. It is a predetermined matter of preference, so "Don't push your values on me." William Provine, the Professor of History of Biology at Cornell University says,

1973 was a progressively giant leap into our new secular global world.

"Human free will is nonexistent....free will is a disastrous and mean social myth...therefore it is cruel to prosecute people for crimes." [7]

To explain further, the materialist believes that man is composed of matter. Therefore, our actions are entirely predetermined by that matter (genetics). Morality is preprogrammed by evolution. This, of course, naturally lends itself to the 'victim mentality' which is rampant in our society. "It's not my fault. That's just who I am."

Free will is required for a moral standard to be fair and just. Since there is no free will, there are no moral standards. Since there are no moral standards, then the Bible is not true and there is no sin and there is no judgement. In the 1948 book, which helped spark the sexual revolution, *Sexual Behavior in the Human Male,* Alfred Kinsey makes it clear that people are naturally under the impression that 'if it feels good, do it.'

Their arguments are at most plausible if there is no god. The existence of God provides the only coherent explanation to the necessary conditions of there being an objective morality. [8] One character from famed Russian novelists, Fyodor Dostoyeusky has said, "If God is dead, then all things are permissible." I can assure you, God is not dead. For that reason, all things are not permissible, but thanks be to God, all things are possible!

What does humanistic and materialistic permissiveness do to our moral compass and collective conscience? God has spoken that human life is valuable. To kill an innocent human life is a serious sin.   The Bible records that God created mankind to be higher in worth than other forms of life such as bacteria, shrimp, plants and whales. This was God's standard of moral objectivity. Remove God from his creation and you remove objective moral standards. Humanity loses its God-given human value and distinct dignity. We downgrade the image of God in which we have been made to just another evolved species on the Phylogenetic tree.

The result, activists rally against the unborn's human right to live. They fight against scientifically living humans in the womb while protesting for the rights of animals. Unreservedly, animals deserve protection, care and compassion. Common sense tells us that animal rights are a wonderful and well-intentioned cause. The predicament is the supposed equality of humans and animals. Why? If humans have rights and there is no qualitative difference between a human and an animal, then animals should have rights, too. Furthermore, we kill animals when it suits our purposes or when they are no longer useful, therefore it is permissible to kill humans when it serves our purposes or when they are no longer useful.

Our 'most influential living philosopher,' Peter Singer, confidently lays out the case against the inherent value of human life. "The idea of you being made in the image of some cosmic being is sheer nonsense and that's the only idea that would make you think that you are special. We have to consider eliminating you when you have outlived your usefulness." [9] Additionally, he claims that if we make man into something special we are "speciesist." Such as a racist exalts one race over another, sexist exalts one gender over another; a speciesist is someone who exalts one species "humans" over other animals. The official, and yes, I mean 'official' term is — speciesism. Singer is a proponent of sexual relations between humans and animals. "We are animals" — and the result is that "sex across the species barrier ceases to be an offense to our status and dignity as human beings. [10]

This is not fear based moral science fiction. This is the historical repercussion of Darwinian logic. No God. No morality. No objective standard. No sin. No judgment. Human life has no value. Welcome to the world of Eugenics and Euthanasia. The late Catholic Apologetic, G.K. Chesterton, warned us more than 50 years ago that scientific materialism had become the dominant creed in Western Culture, "beginning with Evolution and ending in Eugenics." [11]

Eugenics means well born. The term was coined in 1883 by Sir Francis Galton, a cousin of Charles Darwin. Positive eugenics was a movement that attempted to "improve" the human population by encouraging "fit" people to reproduce. Negative eugenics, conversely, attempted to "improve" the human population by discouraging "unfit" people from reproducing. The "unfit" people included the poor, the sick, the disabled and the "feeble-minded," the "idiots," the "morons," and the "insane." And "discouragement" from reproducing included the use of force.

Adolf Hitler was infamously known as a proponent of Eugenics, as Nazi scientists practiced rare and painful experiments on imprisoned Jews before the death chamber. Unfortunately, we do not have to look overseas to a mad despot from socialist Europe to find such a small view of the value of human life. America can rightfully claim our own eugenic visionary in Margaret Sanger.

In 1921, Sanger founded the American Birth Control League, which (following a 1939 merger with the Birth Control Clinical Research Bureau and then a 1942 name change) became the Planned Parenthood Federation of America. While the organization was growing, the close association between the birth control movement and the eugenics movement had made a necessary name change. Nazi Germany had implemented racial hygiene policies, including mass sterilizations inspired by the eugenics movement in America. So "birth control" was removed from the name to create a new public image, but the agenda stayed the same. And in 1948, Sanger helped form the International Committee on Planned Parenthood, which (in 1952) became the International Planned Parenthood Federation. [12]

Planned Parenthood was organized to abolish minorities and the poor. In Margaret Sanger's 1922 book, *The Pivot of Civilization,* she attacked charity as counterproductive and dangerous for helping the poor to produce even more "human waste" (her definition of poor children). She wrote, "Organized charity is itself the symptom of a malignant social disease." And, "Instead of decreasing and aiming to eliminate the stocks [of people] that are most detrimental to the future of the race and the world, it tends to render them to a menacing degree dominant." [13] Evidently, this helps to explain why the ratio of Planned Parenthood clinics in urban areas, predominately populated by African-Americans and Hispanics, are two-and-half times more than the amount of clinics located in suburban areas.

The cheerleaders of eugenics are now rallying in the corner of assisted suicide. The proper word is euthanasia, meaning "the painless killing of a patient suffering from an incurable and painful disease or in an irreversible coma." [14]

Brannon Howse defines three categories of euthanasia. "Active euthanasia is another step forward of that sinful thirst to become as gods. We decide when a person dies. This decision is based on complete relevancy of the, so called, quality of life. Passive euthanasia allows nature to take its course. Hospice, etc... Active euthanasia is when a physician hastens death through lethal injection. Voluntary means the patient wanted to die. Involuntary borders homicide." [15] Nature taking its course, in this cursed world, is unavoidable. The goal should be to make it as painless as possible. However, assisting and quickening someone's death is why King David sentenced the Amalekite to death for helping King Saul die, even though Saul requested it (2nd Samuel 1:12-16).

Finally, why is the devaluing of human life and the personal subjective morality which allows physicians to perform abortions and euthanasia becoming all too common? Dr. Howard Hintz, in the *Journal of Higher Education*, details the fact that secular Humanism is a religion. He quotes Dr. Reed Bell in his book, *Prescription Death Compassionate Killers in the Medical Profession*. It describes a bioethics course he attended at Vanderbilt University. "The course taught by

John Lachs was entitled, 'Individual Rights and the Public Good in the Treatment of Humans.' On the first day of class, Lachs encouraged the students to be open-minded about the subject matter and to expect to change their mindset about the practice of medicine. The professor's ethical discourse conveyed the primary message that we should accept as ethical abortion, infanticide, condone suicide and euthanasia. After the first week, says Dr. Bell, I approached the professor and asked him where these new ideas came from for the practice of medicine. He handed me a copy of a Humanist Manifesto II and told me, this was the source of the new ethic. The Bible is censored from the classroom only to be replaced by a new Bible — Humanist Manifestoes I and II and 2000." [16]

Opposing worldviews have denied the Bible as 100% true and God inspired. This denies sin and the objective moral standards God graciously gave us for our benefit through His word. The alternative theory offers predetermined personal morals, no free will to obey repressive religious values and no intrinsic God-given value to human life. The future is looking "bright," as Richard Dawkins prefers to call himself. Science is now unleashed, unlimited and unchecked in human engineering, such as The Human Genome Project, therapeutic cloning, embryonic stem cell research and sex-selective abortions. Science without sin...? Humans without God-given objective moral standards and restraints?

President George Washington strongly warns us, "Let us, with caution, indulge the supposition that morality can be maintained without religion. Reason and experience both forbid us to expect that national morality can prevail in exclusion of religious principle."

Chapter Six

Core Belief #3

The devil is real, not merely a symbolic figure of evil

Revealed Knowledge

You belong to your father, the devil, and you want to carry out
your father's desires. He was a murderer from the beginning,
not holding to the truth, for there is no truth in him.
When he lies, he speaks his native language,
for he is a liar and the father of lies.
John 8:44

Then Jesus was led by the Spirit into the wilderness to be
tempted by the devil. After fasting forty days and forty nights, he
was hungry. The tempter came to him and said,...
Matthew 4:1-3

If Satan drives out Satan, he is divided against himself.
How then can his kingdom stand?
Matthew 12:26

...to open their eyes and turn them from darkness to light, and
from the power of Satan to God...
Acts 26:18

In order that Satan might not outwit us.
For we are not unaware of his schemes.
2 Corinthians 2:11

...in which you used to live when you followed the ways of this world and of the ruler of the kingdom of the air, the spirit who is now at work in those who are disobedient.
Ephesians 2:2

For we wanted to come to you—certainly I, Paul, did, again and again—but Satan blocked our way.
1 Thessalonians 2:18

For this reason, when I could stand it no longer, I sent to find out about your faith. I was afraid that in some way the tempter had tempted you and that our labors might have been in vain.
1 Thessalonians 3:5

Some have in fact already turned away to follow Satan.
1 Timothy 5:15

Submit yourselves, then, to God.
Resist the devil, and he will flee from you.
James 4:7

Be alert and of sober mind. Your enemy the devil prowls around like a roaring lion looking for someone to devour.
Resist him, standing firm in the faith, because you know that the family of believers throughout the world is undergoing the same kind of sufferings.
1 Peter 5:8-9

The one who does what is sinful is of the devil, because the devil has been sinning from the beginning. The reason the Son of God appeared was to destroy the devil's work.
1 John 3:8

We know that we are children of God, and that the whole world is under the control of the evil one.
1 John 5:19

The Lord said to Satan, "Very well, then, everything he has is in
your power, but on the man himself do not lay a finger."
Then Satan went out from the presence of the Lord.
Job 1:12

He replied, "I saw Satan fall like lightning from heaven."
Matthew 10:18

How you are fallen from heaven,
O Lucifer, son of the morning!
How you are cut down to the ground,
You who weakened the nations!
For you have said in your heart:
'I will ascend into heaven,
I will exalt my throne above the stars of God;
I will also sit on the mount of the congregation
On the farthest sides of the north;
I will ascend above the heights of the clouds,
I will be like the Most High.'
Isaiah 14:12-14 NKJV

The great dragon was hurled down—that ancient serpent called
the devil, or Satan, who leads the whole world astray. He was
hurled to the earth, and his angels with him.
Revelation 12:9

Reasons to Know

The local folklore of the Jersey Devil, the mysterious creature that roams the forested Pine Barrens of NJ, devouring chickens and cows has increased with interest in pop culture the past decade. The History Channel, The Travel Channel, and Animal Planet just to name a few, have all covered the winged kangaroo with cloven hooves. There is something about legendary evil and the demonic realm that is intriguing to channel surfers on prime time cable. I, once again, ... digress.

After the relocation of the NJ Nets to Brooklyn, the only professional sports team left with the national designation 'New Jersey,' is the NJ Devils of the National Hockey League. I must say, it is an entirely appropriate name with which to associate New Jersey to the national sports scene.

In 2013, WrestleMania 29 was hosted in NJ at MetLife Stadium but nationally promoted as NY/NJ. In 2014, the Superbowl made its long awaited arrival to a cold climate at MetLife Stadium in NJ. National marketing, graphics and promotion all highlighted the NY/NJ location. Understand the perfect fit for the NJ Devils? New Jersey is often overlooked and so is the devil.

Do not feel sympathy for the Devil as the Rolling Stones sang in their 1968 song. He prefers the under the radar lifestyle, secretly hiding in the shadows. To be overlooked is not an insult. It is a profound compliment of his character and his strategy. There is no spirit realm in the naturalistic worldview. If an individual refuses to overlook the existence of the devil, he is ostracized.

For example, Supreme Court Justice Anthony Scalia told NY Magazine that he believes in the existence of a real personal devil.

Justice Scalia: "I even believe in the Devil."

Jennifer Senior, NY Magazine: "You do?"

Justice Scalia: "Of course! Yeah, he's a real person. Hey, c'mon, that's standard Catholic doctrine! Every Catholic believes that."

Jennifer Senior, NY Magazine: "Every Catholic believes this? There's a wide variety of Catholics out there ..."

Justice Scalia: "If you are faithful to Catholic dogma, that is certainly a large part of it."

Jennifer Senior, NY Magazine: "Have you seen evidence of the Devil, lately?"

Justice Scalia: "You know, it is curious. In the Gospels, the Devil is doing all sorts of things. He's making pigs run off cliffs, he's possessing people and whatnot. And that doesn't happen very much anymore."

Jennifer Senior, NY Magazine: "No."

Justice Scalia: "It's because he's smart."

Jennifer Senior, NY Magazine: "So what's he doing now?"

Justice Scalia: "What he's doing now is getting people not to believe in him or in God. He's much more successful that way."

Jennifer Senior, NY Magazine: "That has really painful implications for atheists. Are you sure that's the Devil's work?"

Justice Scalia: "I didn't say atheists are the Devil's work."

Jennifer Senior, NY Magazine: "Well, you're saying the Devil is persuading people to not believe in God. Couldn't there be other reasons to not believe?"

Justice Scalia: "Well, there certainly can be other reasons. But it certainly favors the Devil's desires. I mean, c'mon, that's the explanation for why there's not demonic possession all over the place. That always puzzled me. What happened to the Devil, you know? He used to be all over the place. He used to be all over the New Testament."

Jennifer Senior, NY Magazine: "Right."

Justice Scalia: "What happened to him?"

Jennifer Senior, NY Magazine: "He just got wilier."

Justice Scalia: "He got wilier."

Jennifer Senior, NY Magazine: "Isn't it terribly frightening to believe in the Devil?"

Justice Scalia: "You're looking at me as though I'm weird. My God! Are you so out of touch with most of America, most of which believes in the Devil? I mean, Jesus Christ believed in the Devil! It's in the Gospels! You travel in circles that are so, so removed from mainstream America that you are appalled that anybody would believe in the Devil! Most of mankind has believed in the Devil, for all of history. Many more intelligent people than you or me have believed in the Devil." [1]

Justice Scalia, an illustrious professional in the field of law, nominated and confirmed to the bench of The United States Supreme Court, felt an awkward stare of disbelief from a magazine journalist who was dumbfounded at the judge's orthodox, spiritual belief in a real devil. The NY Magazine writer's reaction was trumped by Cenk Uygor of the Young Turks, an internet news show on YouTube with 50 million viewers per month. Mr. Uygor's opinion on Justice Scalia's belief in the devil, "We have a lunatic on the court...he is cuckoo for Cocoa Puffs." [2]

To attribute evil to a spiritual being is insane and out of step with today's secular worldview. It makes perfect, logical sense that there is no devil if, as the secularist's never ending chorus belts out, there is no god. The harmonic atheist sings to a slightly different melody that holds a tight fisted blame on any supposed living deity. If there is evil, it is God's fault, not the devil's. How could God be good or all-powerful if evil continues to prevail and derail our human shared experienced? The existence or non-existence of God becomes the scapegoat for the suffering, sin and sicknesses that cruelly plagues our world.

Why is there evil? What causes suffering? Some place the burden on God. Others, more proficient in casting blame, point the finger of guilt at society: government, corporations, and "the system." The answer is more personal than what many believe or admit. The root is found in each of us. We have all succumbed to the lies and entice-ments of the tempter, Satan himself. The modern great theologian, N.T. Wright believes "The immature reaction of evil is to project evil onto others, generating a culture of blame. It's always everyone else's fault. It's society's fault, it is the government's fault, and I am an in-nocent victim. Claiming the status of the victimized becomes the new multicultural sport." [3]

Neither our earth nor heaven, to our records, knew what iniquity and depravity was until the magnificent and beautiful Lucifer rebelled against God, led one-third of the angels to join his revolt and eventu-ally found himself outside of the Kingdom, banned from the worship of God's throne forever. The angels feebly attempted to hijack God's worship to their own demise. They lost the war and are now a lost cause themselves, with no possible redemption and no possible reconciliation.

Lucifer, better known by his new 'street name,' Satan, was not done. He was cast to the earth and found his coiled secret place in the garden. There he provoked Eve with the same charisma, charm and witty suggestions that the angels foolishly obeyed. The devil foreknew that he could not win against God on earth; he had already been so convincingly beaten. Satan was far more sinister and wise. He was de-feated in the attempt to take God's heaven so, instead, set his heights on breaking God's heart. Objective: cause a curse upon the only cre-ation made in God's image — man. The curse of sin would equal death.

The Devil understood God. He was, for the most part and in hu-man terms, part of God's inner circle of archangels: Michael, Gabriel and Lucifer. The God of life could only be wounded through a dramatic measure, unknown and never experienced by the eternal ministering spirits — death. Angels look in jealously at our salvation, but bemoan the thought of facing death. Nothing would puncture God's heart with greater pain than invading the material world created with pure perfection and replacing the serene with chaos and corruption. A physical world with heaven-like qualities: no death, no decay, no disease, would now meet the love of God and the wrath of God.

To summarize, there is evil in the earth because there is a curse upon this earth, caused by sin and rebellion. This is the Devil's work and he is a true professional. The Devil is a liar and a murderer. These are two separate adjectives of identity and describe his one goal — spiritual death and physical death but death nonetheless. The existence of death is the single most accomplished career goal of this ruthless rebel, including the woeful death of the first Adam and the willful death of the second Adam. Death itself, the enemy of man, is traced back to man's greatest enemy and his most attractive adversary — The Satan, the Devil.

How should we, in modern society, address the notion of evil and the demonic? Quoting again, N.T. Wright, "C.S. Lewis and his famous Screwtape Letters, suggested that there were two equal and opposite errors into which people could fall when they thought about the Devil. One hand, they might take him to seriously; imagining Satan equal to and opposite to God or to Jesus, and seeing Satanic influence and activity behind every problem and misfortune. The opposite error is for people to sneer or mock the very idea of the demonic. I suggest there's a further error. There's a danger that we suppose all such language to be merely the projection onto a fictitious maybe 'mythological' screen of those aspects of our own personalities and psyches. Carl Jung has tried to urge that we should learn to befriend our 'shadow side' and see what we presently call 'evil' or what we presently shun as satanic is simply another aspect — perhaps a very creative and hence threatening one of our full-orbed personality." [4]

The Devil is real but do not blame him directly for every tooth ache or traffic jam. Yet, do not discount him when a tooth ache leads to a life threatening infection in an otherwise perfectly healthy man. Do not dismiss him when that traffic jam is caused by a drunk driving accident. There are physical ailments involved in medical emergencies and cause and effect principles in each accident. The point is to recognize the work of the Devil in conjunction with the free will choices of man. In Core Belief #4, Saved by Grace, we will learn that wrongdoing continues due to man's inherent fallen, corrupt nature. However, Satan is still working behind-the-scenes with mind games described as schemes and devices in most New Testament translations (2 Cor 2:11). His method of expertise in tempting man to commit diabolical actions, always with death in mind, is matchless and merciless. The constant bombardment of unspoken, confidentially heard, inner thoughts of jealousy, rage, sexual fulfillment and pride makes Satan the most prominent master of puppets.

The fact remains, the devil is not equal to God. He is not omnipresent (everywhere at once), omnipotent (all-powerful) or omniscient (all-knowing). He uses a hierarchy of demons that are assigned to activities. These demonic forces are the one-third of fallen angels led astray by Satan. Now as their chief, he operates within this physical sphere through their spiritual influence.

Currently, Satan wars against God and His people; a repeated theme in all of Scripture. In the Old Testament, Pharaoh wanted to keep God's people in bondage. Today, the Devil wants to keep people in spiritual bondage as slaves to sin.

Reality Known

All opposing worldviews attribute moral evil, such as the actions of men, separate from natural evil, such as hurricanes and earthquakes. These views say that men have been predetermined by genetics and environment to act certain ways that other evolved humans may find morally offensive. This moral difference is a genetic difference or in some cases, an environmental cultural difference. Not, as religious undertones would surmise, a choice of absolute good or absolute evil because there are no absolutes. Everything is relative. Review Core Belief #2 for further insight. The Garden of Eden debunks this myth. Adam and Eve had perfect genetics. They lived in a perfect environment and had the perfect Father figure, God Himself. Yet they willingly disobeyed and made a dreadful decision. Decisions have consequences.

Our view of government and church gels at this intersection of good and evil.

The government has a direct sovereign role and responsibility to stop evil actions. Using force to prevent or punish 'evildoers' is essential for Law and Order in a world of immorality and chaos.

> Let everyone be subject to the governing authorities, for
> there is no authority except that which God has established.
> The authorities that exist have been established by God.
> Consequently, whoever rebels against the authority is rebelling
> against what God has instituted, and those who do so will bring
> judgment on themselves. For rulers hold no terror for those who
> do right, but for those who do wrong. Do you want to be free
> from fear of the one in authority? Then do what is right and you
> will be commended. For the one in authority is God's servant
> for your good. But if you do wrong, be afraid, for rulers do not
> bear the sword for no reason. They are God's servants, agents
> of wrath to bring punishment on the wrongdoer. Therefore, it
> is necessary to submit to the authorities, not only because of
> possible punishment but also as a matter of conscience.
> **Romans 13:1-5**

God has granted the state, a.k.a the government, the power to protect its citizens from the evil actions and plans of others in society. A civilized and peaceful world is heaven's mercy on a cursed hell-bent planet. Review the thoughts of our Founding Fathers:

Our view of government and church gels at this intersection of good and evil.

"Society in every state is a blessing, but government, even in its best state, is but a necessary evil; in its worst state an intolerable one; for when we suffer or are exposed to the same miseries by a government, which we might expect in a country without government, our calamity is heightened by reflecting that we furnish the means by which we suffer." — **Thomas Paine, Common Sense 1776**

"It has been said that all government is an evil. It would be more proper to say that the necessity of any government is a misfortune. This necessity however exists; and the problem to be solved is, not what form of government is perfect, but which of the forms is least imperfect." — **James Madison, to an unidentified correspondent 1833**

"Why has government been instituted at all? Because the passions of men will not conform to the dictates of reason and justice
without constraint." — **Alexander Hamilton, Federalist No. 1**5

Government, including democracies, are not perfect because such
government, even that which is "for the people and by the people," are
administered by sinful, corrupt, elected leaders who are representing
immoral dishonest citizens. That is a fair assessment on why democracies collapse, though much preferred over monarchies and totalitarian
regimes. They offer freedom but not perfection in government.

Graciously, God has temporarily given the power of the sword to
the state to punish people and prevent crimes. According to Paine,
Madison and Hamilton, the primary role of government is a necessary
and misfortunate evil in itself but required because the "sinful" passions of men will not submit to reason without forced restraint.

The Church has been given the greater power of the Word or
spiritual sword (Hebrews 4:12, Matthew 10:34). Government is God's
administration on earth to restrain man. The Church is God's administration on earth to regenerate man. Hence, Jesus commanded us to
visit those in prison (Matthew 25:36). The Government does its job in
incarcerating criminals, if legally found guilty, We, as the Church, must
do our job and offer them the truth of the gospel to be "born again."
Civil laws do not entirely stop wickedness as God's Law did not stop sin.
Regeneration, not restraint, will fundamentally stop evil by inwardly
and eternally changing the man.

The nonreligious world rejects the gospel of Christ as the means
to a healthy community. We have been told that our problems are not
spiritual nor evil in nature. The devil has been replaced with genetics
and environmental causes.

Dr. Philip Zimbardo, in his book *The Lucifer Effect*, says when
there is evil, the question is not who is responsible but what is responsible. His observations conclude, there are sometimes bad apples
(inwardly bad people through evolutionary genetics), sometimes bad
barrels (external conditions the person is influenced by) and finally, bad
barrel makers (the political, economical and legal systems that create
the external conditions). Zimbardo concludes, pertaining to the answer
of depraved actions in our world, that to change the person, you change
the situation, to change the situation, you change the system.

The false crutch of liberal societies are their aspirations in using government public policies to improve individuals. Evil is not an unfortunate consequence of cultural and shared community environments. Evil is in the heart of man. When tempted to perform actions that violate the moral objective standards of God, evil travels from the heart of that man into the destructive power of the hand of that man. Ineffectively, the social progressive policies have worsened the condition of liberty, both politically and spiritually. Billions of dollars have been delegated over decades to improving underprivileged communities, offer more opportunities, better schools, and social service tracks to success. For all that, we as a collective society, tragically double down on the rights of sexual expression, violent excessiveness in entertainment and situational ethics in public education. The conscience of man is constantly corrupting while we theoretically propose new social ideas.

> The nonreligious world rejects the gospel of Christ as the means to a healthy community. We have been told that our problems are not spiritual nor evil in nature. The devil has been replaced with genetics and environmental causes.

I believe most pastors and politicians fail to remember why religious organizations are tax exempt. Sure, there is a Biblical precedent, but the government at one time recognized the work the Church accomplished by morally developing better, more productive citizens, which then required less legal restraint and tax investment. The less influential the Church is, the more dominant the government becomes. As the theme of this book communicates, if your humanist, atheist and statist dream is to have a centralized, integrated, secular, authoritative government which connects the world as one, then the prescribed course of action is to weaken the Church and the religion of the people. As faith decreases, evil will increase. More government jurisdiction, better marketed as our collective salvation, will be mandatory for our survival.

Chapter Seven

Core Belief #4
Man is sinful and saved by grace

Revealed Knowledge

There is no one righteous, not even one...for all have sinned
and fallen short of God's glory.
Romans 3:10, 23

...and all are justified freely by his grace through the
redemption that came by Christ Jesus.
Romans 3:24

You were dead in your sins...among whom we all once
lived in the passions of our flesh, carrying out the desires of the
body and the mind, and were by nature children of wrath,
like the rest of mankind.
Ephesians 2:1,3

For it is by grace you have been saved, through faith—and this
is not from yourselves, it is the gift of God.
Ephesians 2:8

The Lord saw how great the wickedness of the human race had
become on the earth, and that every inclination of the thoughts
of the human heart was only evil all the time.
Genesis 6:5

But Noah found (grace) favor in the eyes of the Lord.
author added the parenthetical for emphasis **Genesis 6:8**

Therefore, just as sin entered the world through one man, and
death through sin, and in this way death came to all people,
because all sinned.
Romans 5:12

So that, just as sin reigned in death,
so also grace might reign through righteousness to bring eternal
life through Jesus Christ our Lord.
Romans 5:21

The Lord smelled the pleasing aroma and said in his heart:
"Never again will I curse the ground because of humans,
even though every inclination of the human heart is evil from
childhood."
Genesis 8:21

I say then: Walk in the Spirit, and you shall not fulfill the lust
of the flesh. For the flesh lusts against the Spirit, and the Spirit
against the flesh; and these are contrary to one another, so that
you do not do the things that you wish.
Galatians 5:16-17

Surely I was sinful at birth,
sinful from the time my mother conceived me.
Psalm 51:5

Reasons to Know

The storytellers of our age are fascinated with redemption in the
lives of fictional characters on the big screen. Hollywood can
create plots and personalities that are emotional, engaging and
inspiring; they can make a dog cry over a cat. The audience loves the
resurrection moment about two-thirds through the movie, normally
involving the relationship of the romantic, leading man and lady, or
the school teacher with a young potential leader. The odds seem too
great. The shortcomings of the main character, too much to overcome.
Humility and fear convinces the superhero or the pacifist front runner

to give in, count your losses, and accept your fate of failure. One kiss or one motivational talk changes everything. In the end, the dialogue is different in each script, the background production music will vary but without question, the handsome stud gets the girl and the scared leader saves the day.

Collections and montages of inspirational movie moments are easily searched on Youtube. The foremost call to action is to "believe in yourself." Christian parents have, themselves, been indoctrinated with the self-esteem campaigns of the 1970s and 1980s, partnered with the upbringing of Disney movies babysitting our attention. We ignorantly instruct our children, "believe in yourself," "follow your heart," "you can do whatever you set your mind to."

For many, such comforting words of elementary encouragement is Class One of Parenting 101. However, the heart that our child follows is deceitful (Jeremiah 17:9) and sinful. The mind that we set our goals on is not renewed but carnal and leads to death. By teaching children to believe in themselves, we have obliviously trained them as Deists.

Humanism has transformed Christians into practical atheists.

Though we might believe in God, we live as though he does not exist. Not in the works of the flesh but our insistence to be what we want to be, following our desires, choosing our path, chasing our dream, believing in ourselves — all of this absent from the oversight, will and sovereignty of God. Unless, of course, in religious duty, we ask God to bless our predetermined plan.

Fully baptized in Hollywood ideology, we can save the world, save ourselves and save the environment. Void of the knowledge of our impotence, we are vexed with the delusion of our importance. Our self-imposed wonderfulness has out-dueled our miserable wretchedness.

A biblical worldview teaches that man is made in the image of God. Man is a spirit, possesses a soul and lives in a body. Man has intrinsic worth and value, and is the highest form of life in all of God's creation. Yet, man is naturally born with an inherent sinful nature. Man is in need of regeneration. His actions are connected to his internal spiritual problem, not an external physical problem.

Humanism has transformed Christians into practical atheists.

Blaise Pascal, the famed philosopher, has rightly pointed out our duality. "What sort of freak than is man?... We are the glory and the garbage of the universe!" Christianity understands both the glory of the creation of man and the reality of his fallen nature. Allow me to define us as such — we are everything that is great in the world and everything that is wrong in the world. Call the government, call the universities, call the think-tank organizations, call Google; we stumbled upon what is wrong in the world and the answer is us.

Incorrectly, the opposing worldviews teach that man is a purely physical being who is basically good but influenced by his environment. If man is able to correct his environment, man himself would be different. If man's surroundings were improved, evil would become non-existent or minimized. Some believe man has no value, as he is only a natural being made of matter. Others consider man a self-god, able to achieve great pleasure and fulfillment in this life through self-actualization.

To further explain the biblical description of man, we can accurately categorize man into three states of existence. The first state of man was Innocence. The holy and pure creative masterpiece placed in the Garden of Eden by Elohim, God our creator. Theologians cannot concur how long man was in this state of innocence but for six thousands years or more, we have longed to return. The second state of man can be categorized as Fallen. Immediately, after Adam and Eve committed high treason in the untainted garden, mankind separated himself from God as the guilt of a wounded and ashamed conscience drove him away in fear. Man, who was proudly made 'in the image of God' is now described in these awful terms: evil, spiritually dead, blind, deaf, lost, rebellious, haters of God, children of the Devil, children of wrath...just to name a few. Finally, the third state of man is gloriously titled, the Redeemed State. Pick up your heads, as Jesus said, and view these new and improved terms describing men who live in the Redeemed State: the redeemed, saints, priests, the people of God, a holy nation, royal priesthood, children of God, sons of God, beloved. It is consoling and comforting to have our resurrection and redeeming moment without the Hollywood fanfare, so saturated in humanistic overlays.

Ravi Zacharias, on his radio broadcast *Let My People Think,* gives us a practical view of our current fallen state, "Prosperity does not make piety. Morally, we are sensual. Socially, we are violent. Physically, we are diseased. Spiritually, we are empty."

The effects of sin is all encompassing throughout life, according to Rod Parsley, "From the womb we suffer under its congenital effects. It separates our hearts from His heart. It causes us to go left when we know we should go right. It's what makes us accept the counterfeit as real, and reject the real as counterfeit. It drives us to our destruction. It makes us say what we shouldn't want to say and go where we shouldn't want to go and do what we shouldn't want to do. It compels us to hurt, use and abuse the very ones we should love and serve." [1]

Dinesh D'Souza concurs, "Sin structures our personalities and defines our thoughts and behavior. Sin is built into our habits so that we sin routinely, almost unthinkingly. Sin is not peripheral to humans, something we occasionally do but is much more intrinsic to our identities." [2]

Collectively and individually, we project moral failures on others or simply disregard any moral code as absolute and objective, thus removing ourselves from conviction. This lack of the 'need to change' justifies man's conscience. If humanists and materialists are correct and man is predetermined through evolutionary genetics then man cannot change. Hence, man cannot repent for his actions for his actions are not a moral choice. He does what he is!

Music queen Lady Gaga sings with a false confidence and celebration of who she is, in the popular song *Born This Way*, lyrics edited:

No matter gay, straight or bi
Lesbian, transgendered life
I'm on the right track, baby...
I'm beautiful in my way
'Cause God makes no mistakes

I'm on the right track, baby
I was born this way...[3]

Without question, God makes no mistakes! Surely, man does! The result is a perfect creation, full of unlimited potential during that short lived State of Innocence, now born in a sinful Fallen State. We are not 'on the right track,' per Gaga but on the 'wrong track.' If, indeed, you are 'born this way,' you must, per Jesus Christ, be 'born again.'

Enter through the narrow gate. For wide is the gate and broad
is the road that leads to destruction, and many enter through it.
But small is the gate and narrow the road that leads to life,
and only a few find it.
Matthew 7:13-14

Very truly I tell you, no one can see the kingdom of God
unless they are born again.
John 3:3

Forgive my boorish belief in sin but it is the silent and often undetected killer of humanity. Scientists wrestle with viruses, bacteria and mutations as we 'run for the cures' and raise money for research. Hidden, not in the microscopes of university labs but in the heart of man, is the greatest and oldest source of death; sin itself. Research is not the answer. Repentance is.

Famed rapper, Macklemore word dances in similar fashion with his song *Same Love*. Appealing to predetermined evolutionary genetics, he persuades the young listener to question religion; not your sinful nature. The use of such justification earned this song the platform of the 2014 Grammy Awards, when a host of couples, both straight and same-sex, married each other by the power invested in Queen Latifah. Lyrics edited:

The right wing conservatives think it's a decision
And you can be cured with some treatment and religion
Man-made rewiring of a predisposition...
And I can't change
Even if I tried
Even if I wanted to
And I can't change [4]

Evolutionary ethics, once the brainchild of university philosophers, has been translated into the language of the adolescent by performers. In the book, *Demonic Males: Apes and the Origins of Human Violence*, the authors claim that even the Sept 11th terrorist attacks had nothing to do with moral evil, but their predisposition to violence "is written in the molecular chemistry of DNA." It is the unoriginal 'my genes made me do it' excuse. To further our non-suggestive reading list, the book, *The Natural History of Rape: Biological Bases of Sexual Coercion*, supports the theory that forced intercourse is not morally evil, but an evolutionary benefit that our genes are wired to procreate. [5]

All desires which humanity possesses this day, no matter how incomprehensible and logically gross, are beneficial and acceptable because they survived evolution's natural selection process. Moral freedom and human dignity is non-existent in evolutionary morality. In the book, *The Moral Animal*, Robert Wright argues, "our genes control us" and that, "free will is an illusion," part of an "outdated worldview." [6]

Thus, repentance is not possible and worse, it's suppressive as it demands a change of thought that through the grace of God, will lead to a change in action. Repentance is theoretically anti-evolution.

Humanists declare such traditional rhetoric is restrictive religious dogma.

Repent, for the kingdom of heaven has come near.
Matthew 3:2

From that time on Jesus began to preach,
"Repent, for the kingdom of heaven has come near."
Matthew 4:17

They went out and preached that people should repent.
Mark 6:12

I have not come to call the righteous, but sinners to repentance.
Luke 5:32

I tell you, no! But unless you repent, you too will all perish.
Luke 13:3

Reality Known

The tragedy of our age is the false philosophy 'free will does not exist.' Morality is predetermined, not chosen. Sin does not exist, for there is no moral objective standard by which humanity will be judged, for there is no god. Therefore, the logical conclusion built on the incorrect assumption, or starting point, is as follows: People believe that if I am born this way, then it must be natural (of nature) and if natural then it must be good and beneficial because the desires are part of my genetic makeup, which has survived the process of evolution. Therefore, if such genetic desires remain with us today, then they must be for a good reason as these genes were not eliminated through

> Thus, repentance is not possible and worse, it's suppressive as it demands a change of thought that through the grace of God, will lead to a change in action. Repentance is theoretically anti-evolution.

natural selection. In other words, if a person is born with a desire, then that desire has been genetically deposited there by uncontrollable, evolutionary processes. Don't judge and don't push your evolutionary values on me. Worse, evolutionary ethics are founded upon the theory of macro evolution which rests upon the evidence of transitional fossils, that happen not to exist!

Of course, everyone realizes that this course of logic only applies to sexual liberation and experimentation. Even that is limited to fornication and/or homosexuality. Society still enforces and imposes their moral standards on adulterers, pedophiles, incest relationships and bestiality. All of these can be viewed as genetic desires which have survived natural selection and to which no moral objective standard exists to object to these moral decisions. The following moral uncertainty leaves an unanswered question — without an objective standard, who decides which genetics are desires and which are disorders?

Subjective morality, highly celebrated in theory, fails miserably in practice. A nation of law and order is a judicial and legal system of forced morality for the common good. Despite proposed genetics of animal kinship it is still clear that sexual aggression, sex trafficking, rape and child pornography are not allowed. Moral relativism will forever be unexplainable and confusing.

Today in our world, it is unfair and intolerant to propose the idea that a person's identity is separate from his actions. A person cannot repent and change. Gaga says, "I was born this way." However, that is not the argument. The debate is whether you must be that way.

For example, a person might believe they are born gay. Genetics does not confirm this and in some cases, such as twins, who share the same DNA but have different sexual preferences and orientations, science denies it. However, being born with a certain desire which feels completely natural does not change the person's identity. Man is made in the image of God as a male or female, and is unconditionally loved by the Creator. Through a natural born fallen nature, including sinful, sexual desires, a male or female might struggle with same sex attraction or any of the sexual choices which fall under the Greek word *porneo* — root word for pornography. In this instance, the individual still remains a male or female. Their desire, attraction and temptation is a separate moral choice of action, not their personal identity. Today's culture demands a different verdict. A person's sexual desire or sexuality has become their identity.

In another failure of moral relativism, an individual is celebrated for changing their gender identity, such as famed Olympian and reality TV star Bruce Jenner. Yet, individuals are discredited for claiming to have changed their sexual orientation. In New Jersey, such conversion therapy is increasingly becoming illegal. [7]

The Apostle Peter illustrates that man is fallen and passing away. Man must be born again, not enlightened or educated to fulfill his inner desire through self actualization. How? Through social programs, government intervention, french philosopher Rousseau's big government, Humanist Manifesto's 'save ourselves' global world dream? The answer is no. Man can be changed and saved through the word of God.

> For you have been born again, not of perishable seed, but of imperishable, through the living and enduring word of God. "For, All people are like grass, and all their glory is like the flowers of the field; the grass withers and the flowers fall, but the word of the Lord endures forever." And this is the word that was preached to you.
> **1 Peter 1:23-25**

Understanding the real nature of man and his relationship to God, is the primary component in handling the difficulties of our shared existence in local, regional and national communities. Admitting man is essentially depraved, sinful and in need of regeneration will guide us in our social sciences; specifically, in the difference between what the government can attempt with good intentions, compared to what the Church can accomplish with proven results and divine commissioning. Clearly, modern liberalism, in the form of twentieth century American politics, has substantiated the fact that local neighborhoods and families will not change by social engineering, social programs or social services.

Communities are worse off when the Church becomes the small arm of a large government. Similarly, secular non profits and government agencies labor endlessly to provide felt needs and temporary assistance but fail in God's mission; to make disciples and 'teach them what I have taught you.' The dire and dismal result is, the gospel loses its power and the community loses its hope. Acts of compassion are part of the gospel package and we are our brother's keeper but such good works cannot change man. We were born that way and we must be born again! I have firsthand experience through my own testimony what God does within a man who repents and places his faith in Christ. Hope and change is possible when its personal.

Abandoned to our intellect and tax revenue, our government is feverishly trying to administrate and manage three hundred million sinful, fallen, corrupt citizens whose inner nature is personally wrestling with their own consciousness. School taxes continually sore to newer heights and unsustainable local levels as our optimistic future is invested in better teachers and better technologies. We have new buildings, new computers, new curriculums, but the graduation rate and the college preparation rate stays stagnant.

Public education misses the mark on the most important aspect of training a child, which is the nature of that child. There are particular learning types and physiological differences in groups of children but one constant — the child's inherent sinful nature.

The earliest days of education in the new colonies of America featured the first textbook, *The New England Primer.* It was the most successful educational textbook published in eighteenth century America and it became the foundation of most schooling before the 1790s.[8] The most well known feature was its reliability upon Bible names and teachings to instruct students in the alphabet, vowels, consonants, and syllables. The Puritan faith and practice could be easily noticed in the woodcuts, along with the sin and salvation theologies throughout the book.

Contradictory, in 1690, the same year *The New England Primer* was published, another book *Essay Concerning Human Understanding* by John Locke was published. Locke denied original sin and argued the idea that a child is born as a blank slate. The child's slate can be written through education and experience. Such a suggestion would revolutionize teaching philosophies. Students were no longer viewed as born with a built-in sinful nature but a blank slate. Thereupon, was the great mistake. The schools, through the influence of Locke, misunderstood the nature of a child. Removing prayer and the Ten Commandments has multiplied this error into our current public school debacle of violence, illicit sex and drug abuse. At the very least, if a child was a 'blank slate,' our refusal to write purity, virtue and self-control on that slate has led to undisciplined behaviors.

Moving on to our current state of affairs, sin has its short term benefits and its long term consequences. I will place these under the defining headers of radical individualism and radical egalitarianism, briefly mentioned in Chapter 1. The so-called personal benefits are more sarcastic than factual.

The lust for sexual freedom without moral restraint or responsibility has been conceived in the corrupt heart of man since Genesis. However, our 'coming out' party happened during the 1960s Sexual Revolution. Lawlessness ripped across our universities as radical individualism sparked a culture war. The perceived personal liberty of 'if it feels good do it,' deceitfully ushered in the fall back plan of superpower federal overreach and progressive government. Strictly speaking, a radical egalitarian government that lacked the will power to enforce moral laws, such as pornography, marriage and abortion regulations but was more than happy to increase its jurisdiction over the economy. My conservative principles are grieved but I must admit, and independent libertarians must concede the lack of moral restraint equals the growth of government.

Where there is no revelation, people cast off restraint; but
blessed is the one who heeds wisdom's instruction.
Proverbs 29:18

If people have no revealed knowledge from God or moral objective standards, they will inevitably cast off restraints (radical individualism).

The King James Version translates 'cast off restraint' as 'they perish.' Both scholarly works are correct. For when one has no moral restraint, one ultimately perishes. What is the default response of a nation to its people who are morally unrestrained and perishing? More government, more programs and more control (radical egalitarianism). I am not alone, Benjamin Franklin bears witness with caution, "Only a virtuous people are capable of freedom. As nations become corrupt and vicious, they have more need of masters." To paraphrase: more sin = more government.

Again, we are soberly faced with the utopian goal thoroughly covered in Chapter 3.

Deny and cripple religion with its suppressive moral standards by condemning and censuring the core beliefs of the Christian faith. Replace religion with secular reasoning and its unaccountable, subjective morality. After the moral restraints are removed, the people will begin to perish.

Then, and only then, will those born in freedom bow down to tyranny to 'save ourselves' through progressive political ideologies.

In conclusion, why is there evil in the world and if there is an all-powerful good God, why doesn't He stop the suffering? Evil is in the heart of man. To destroy inner wickedness, sadly, man must be judged and destroyed. The story of Noah covers this

> Deny and cripple religion with its suppressive moral standards by condemning and censuring the core beliefs of the Christian faith. Replace religion with secular reasoning and its unaccountable, subjective morality. After the moral restraints are removed, the people will begin to perish.

endearing theological and philosophical hair pulling question. God did not remap natural resources to improve primitive economies, to then improve man's actions through a more opportunistic environment. Instead, God wiped out man to wipe out evil. Instantaneously, Noah sinned after the flood and man reproduced as malicious and malevolent as before. To be certain, God will again hold man accountable for his evil actions, and more so, his refusal to confess and repent of his sinful nature. At that Great White Throne Judgement, evil will be bound and the earth will be made new.

Chapter Eight

Core Belief #5
Jesus is the sinless Savior, the Son of God

Revealed Knowledge

The Son (JESUS) is the radiance of God's glory and the exact representation of his being, sustaining all things by his powerful word. After he had provided purification for sins, he sat down at the right hand of the Majesty in heaven.
Hebrews 1:3

The Son (JESUS) is the image of the invisible God, the firstborn over all creation. For in him all things were created: things in heaven and on earth, visible and invisible, whether thrones or powers or rulers or authorities; all things have been created through him and for him. He is before all things, and in him all things hold together.
Colossians 1:15-17

"Don't you know me, Philip, even after I have been among you such a long time? Anyone who has seen me has seen the Father. How can you say, 'Show us the Father'?"
Jesus in John 14:9

The one who looks at me is seeing the one who sent me.
Jesus in John 12:45

For this reason they tried all the more to kill him; not only was he breaking the Sabbath, but he was even calling God his own Father, making himself equal with God.
John 5:18

"Very truly I tell you," Jesus answered, "before Abraham was born, I am!" At this, they picked up stones to stone him, but Jesus hid himself, slipping away from the temple grounds.
John 8:58-59

For we do not have a high priest who is unable to empathize with our weaknesses, but we have one who has been tempted in every way, just as we are—yet he did not sin.
Hebrews 4:15

Such a high priest truly meets our need—
one who is holy, blameless, pure, set apart from sinners,
exalted above the heavens.
Hebrews 7:26

God made him who had no sin to be sin for us, so that in him we might become the righteousness of God.
2 Corinthians 5:21

But you know that he appeared so that he might take away our sins. And in him is no sin.
1 John 3:5

He committed no sin, and no deceit was found in his mouth.
1 Peter 2:22

Reasons to Know

He is internationally known; an icon. His fame and followers transcend generations and cultures. The name is noticeable. Jesus? No, we will get to him. Globe trotting around the world, with stops at the United Nations, The Tonight Show, and African villages, U2's Bono, has used his status to call the world back to good for decades but now, more publicly, he is calling the world back to God.

Bono came to Christ in Ireland during the strife and struggle between Catholics and Protestants. His band, U2, gradually evolved from Christian undertones at their launch, to Christian uncertainty at their peak. Bono, at one time 'could not find what he was looking for.' Traveling the world over and dialoging with leaders who represent unique cultures and belief systems, Bono has come to realize that Jesus' divinity outshines the beliefs and religious dogmas offered worldwide. There is no god, like our God.

In 2005 Bono said, "I ask myself a question a lot of people have asked: Who is this Jesus? Was he who he said he was, or was he just a religious nut?...That's the question." [1] Bono was soul searching. I hold such a quest for truth with upmost respect. He, unlike others, was asking the question,'who is Jesus?' This was a question that needed to be resolved.

In 2013, a recent discussion with Focus on the Family showed a solidified faith with signs of an evangelistic fervor. Bono stated, "When people say good teacher, prophet, really nice guy ... this is not how Jesus thought of himself... So, you're left with a challenge in that, which is either Jesus was who he said he was or a complete and utter nut case. And I believe that Jesus was, you know, the Son of God." [2]

The personhood and Godhood of Jesus is not open for interpretation. His message was too clear to muddle in the doubt of superficial spiritual babble. Jesus is who he says he is or he is who we say he is. Jesus claimed to be God and Jesus was a man. We can deny that or we can accept that but we cannot reinterpret that. Receive him or reject him but do not dare to reinvent him. Bono, decisively, answered the question posed by Jesus himself, "Who do men say that I am?"

To be honest, men widely differ in their judgement of Jesus. I fully surrender to Him as my Lord and Savior. There are others who willfully stir up uncertainty and unbelief, as they portray a dissimilar Jesus than what historical orthodox Christianity believes and preaches.

Perhaps the ambiguity towards Jesus' god-man nature is due to modern scholars who have discovered new, alternative writings through archeology in the past sixty years. These include the *Gospel of Peter*, *Gospel of Mary*, *Gospel of Thomas*, the *Gospel of Judas*, and the *Secret Gospel of Mark*. These false gospels hold a heretical relevance and

equality in the eyes of scholars who say they are just as historically rich
and accurate as the more accepted biblical accounts.

Not only do these 'alternative' writings disagree with the canonized gospels in Scripture but they contradict themselves. For instance,
Jesus denies he is the Son of God in one of the books and defines
himself as a man who embodies God's spirit (but not god in likeness).
One false gospel states that any man can attain this new god-like spirit
through seeking the spiritual nature of man and escaping the material
world. The secret gospel of Mark suggest that Jesus had sexual sins.

To further discredit them, often times these 'false gospels' find
their source in places outside of Jerusalem. Scholars say these gospels
lack cultural understanding in recounting events that don't match-up
with the culture details of Jesus' day; such as Jewish burial laws.

Unfortunately, something so unhistorical receives regular airplay
on the History Channel or other cable networks. Scholars and Masters
of Divinity orally document the different Jesus, giving credibility to
un-credible sources. The innocent channel surfer stumbles upon five
minutes of intelligent, uninterrupted blasphemy before the commercial
brake moves him onto something more entertaining and engaging. The
damage is done. Faith is weakened. Christ is questioned.

These scholars are risking a greater, more demanding judgement
for their scrupulous opinions and downright assumptions. Most assur-
edly, these gospels are not well received by most experts. Only those
who hold a certain bias against the Jesus of the Bible. Their books
might carry weight for those on the fringe of true scholarship. However,
under close examination, the so-called facts are impossible, baseless
ideas.

Famed vampire author, Ann Rice, recently recommitted herself to
Christ and, had this to say about the top-selling book sales which speak
of a different Jesus in her book *Christ the Lord, Out of Egypt.* Based
on these newly discovered gospels, Rice says, "Arguments about Jesus
himself were full of conjecture. Some books were no more than assumptions piled upon assumptions. Absurd conclusions were reached
on the basis of little or no data at all." [3]

These alternative gospels are not new to the battle of faith. For
this reason in 325AD, at the Council of Nicaea, the Bishops ruled
that the approved inspired writings must agree to the traditional faith
which is found in the four biblical accounts. Stories about Jesus were

circulating throughout the ancient world and false teachers were everywhere. The modern Church should not sweat what has already been settled.

> Evidently some people are throwing you into confusion and are
> trying to pervert the gospel of Christ. But even if we or an angel
> from heaven should preach a gospel other than the one we
> preached to you, let them be under God's curse!
> As we have already said, so now I say again: If anybody is
> preaching to you a gospel other than what you accepted,
> let them be under God's curse!
> **Galatians 1:7-9**

From famed singers to poor one-sided scholarship, who do you say Jesus is? C.S. Lewis has been often quoted from his book *Mere Christianity*, "A man who was merely a man and said the sort of things Jesus said would not be a great moral teacher. He would either be a lunatic — on the level with a man who says he is a poached egg — or he would be the devil of hell. You must make your choice. Either this was, and is, the Son of God, or else a madman or something worse. You can shut him up for a fool or you can fall at his feet and call him Lord and God. But let us not come with any patronizing nonsense about him being a great human teacher. He has not left that open to us."

If Jesus was merely a teacher, conservatively, he was the worst of failures. In three years he raised, trained, and empowered the most deceitful spokesmen who changed the course of the world with a monumental lie. The Apostles preached a message of an unrivaled divine Messiah, who if in reality, was nothing more than a simple Jewish rabbi, then these men created the greatest lie ever told. Seems unlikely to me.

Second, what if Jesus flat out lied. There have been cult-like, charismatic leaders who claimed divine status and were willing, not only to give up their own lives but the lives of their persuaded followers to maintain that lie. The undeniable success of the gospel, makes this theory improbable as well. Remember what Gamaliel the Pharisee said:

> "Men of Israel, consider carefully what you intend to do to
> these men. Some time ago Theudas appeared, claiming to
> be somebody, and about four hundred men rallied to him. He

was killed, all his followers were dispersed, and it all came to
nothing. After him, Judas the Galilean appeared in the days
of the census and led a band of people in revolt. He too was
killed, and all his followers were scattered. Therefore, in the
present case I advise you: Leave these men alone! Let them go!
For if their purpose or activity is of human origin, it will fail. But
if it is from God, you will not be able to stop these men; you will
only find yourselves fighting against God."

Acts 5:35-39

Finally, maybe Christ was straight up cray crazy; it is the most
unrealistic scenario offered so far. Perhaps the man genuinely had a
good heart, good intentions and demonstrated many good works but
was offset by a bad chemical imbalance.

The renowned opinions are remarkable but somewhat routine.
Dan Brown, author of the best selling book and movie *The Divinci Code*,
"Jesus was looked upon as a mortal prophet by his followers. A great
and powerful man, but a man nonetheless." Bill O'Reilly's new book
Killing Jesus, was written specifically to separate fact from fiction. The
biblical Jesus, according to cable news #1 show host, might not be the
historical Jesus.

Dr. Michael Brown, a considerable leader and mentor in communicating biblical truth with love and doctrinal soundness, describes
how many Jews believe Paul the Apostle invented our biblical Jesus in
his book, *The Kosher Jesus*. Some Jewish scholars believe that Paul
made Jesus divine and the son of God. Some even said that Paul wasn't
Jewish and lied about being a Pharisee. If you take out the false teaching on Jesus being divine, you must take out the majority of all the
Gospel passages. You must say that these passages were written in later
or that Paul changed the minds of the eyewitnesses. They also say that
Paul said that Jesus came to give his life for the sins of the world on
a spiritual mission not a political mission. So many Jewish rabbis and
theologians want to say that Jesus' mission was political." [4]

Deepak Chopa, CNN commentator and 21-time NY Times Best-
seller, claims another less experienced Jesus in his book, *The Third
Jesus*. According to Dr. Chopa, the first Jesus is the historical Jesus,
"kind, serene, peaceful, loving" and "the keeper of mysteries," but
also "less than consistent." The second Jesus is one who never existed,

an "abstract theological creation," the "foundation of a religion that has proliferated some twenty-thousand sects." The third Jesus, the one championed by Chopra, is the one "who taught his followers how to reach God-consciousness," and this Jesus "is not the savior, not the one and only Son of God." [5]

Raza Aslan made the media rounds in 2013 with his book *The Zealot*. Retelling an otherwise unproven theory, of a Jesus who was a political reformer made into a pacifist preacher to increase his likeability among the Romans who could easily turn him into a deity. "Two thousand years ago, an itinerant Jewish preacher and miracle worker walked across Galilee, gathering followers to establish what he called the Kingdom of God. The revolutionary movement he launched was so threatening to the established order that he was captured, tortured and executed as a state criminal....Jesus' actions and his teachings about the Kingdom of God clearly indicate that he was a follower of the zealot doctrine, which is why he, like so many zealots before and after him, was ultimately executed by Rome for the crime of sedition." [6]

Some Jewish scholars, along with others like Aslan, believe Jesus was a political revolutionary based on the belief of the "Two Swords" theory in Luke 22. Jesus was going to overthrow the Roman government with faith and two swords! Eighty-nine chapters in the gospels and one sentence misconstrues His mission?

Put down the pitchforks and lanterns, simmer down with your rendition of Onward Christian Solider. Jesus never incited violence. In 70AD, when the Jews rebelled against Rome, the Christians did not participate. For 300 years none of the followers of Christ ever committed violence, even when faced with sure death and inhumane persecution. Jesus is the Lamb of God, both in the gospel and twenty-eight times in Revelation.

Above all, what did Jesus say about himself? What did he claim that persuaded his disciples to die for him and his enemies to crucify him? Scottish writer, Thomas Carlyle records, "If it is not superhuman authority that speaks to us here, it is surely superhuman arrogance." [7]

- He claimed titles that only God could have? 39x's-"I AM"
- Taught people to get baptized in the name of the Father and the Son and the Holy Spirit — making himself equal with God (Matthew 28:19)

- Sermon on the Mount, he claimed his word was more power-ful and had more authority than what God told Moses. "you have heard that it was said (law of Moses), but I say...
- He claimed to be eternal and not from this world
- He said to see him physically was to see the invisible God in human form
- He allowed people to worship him, though his disciples and even angels refused worship from others (John 5:23, John 13:13, John 20:28, Matthew 14:33, Luke 5:8)
- He claimed to have the ability to forgive sin (Mark 2:5,10, Luke 7:48-50)
- He claimed that he would be the judge of people, a role only God could fulfill (John 5:21-23, Matthew 25:31-46)
- Crucified because he, a man claimed to be god, "blasphemy" (Matthew 26:65, Mark 14:64, John 10:33)

Bronson Alcott once told Thomas Carlyle that he could honestly use the words of Jesus, "I and the Father are one." Carlyle responded saying, "Yes, but Jesus got the world to believe him." [8] Honestly, no man could utterly transform the world in three years with lies or undiagnosed schizophrenia. He was not a charismatic, cult-like figure or a demented crack pot. He is Lord and God (John 20:28). His exclusive claims to divinity are equally supported by his miraculous works.

The Bible attributes descriptions to him which belong to God. In the Old Testament, God was The Holy One and the King of Glory (Hosea 11:9, Psalm 24). In the New Testament, Jesus is The Holy One and the Lord of Glory (Acts 3:14, 10:36, 1 Cor 2:8). Other verses that reference Jesus as God, in addition to the Revealed Knowledge section of this chapter, include the following:

Prince of peace, Everlasting Father,
Wonderful Counselor, Almighty God...
Isaiah 9:6

Theirs are the patriarchs, and from them is traced the human ancestry of the Messiah, who is God over all, forever praised!
Romans 9:5

But about the Son he says,
"Your throne, O God, will last for ever and ever;
a scepter of justice will be the scepter of your kingdom."
Hebrews 1:8

While we wait for the blessed hope—the appearing of the glory
of our great God and Savior, Jesus Christ...
Titus 2:13

The climax of our faith, the ground on which the entire gospel message stands and the exclusive, authentic, absolute claim to divine lordship is the resurrection of Jesus Christ. The resurrection proves everything! Professor Dr. Daniel Fuller vows to give up his Christian faith if anyone was to produce the bones of Jesus. [9]

And if Christ has not been raised, your faith is futile;
you are still in your sins.
1 Corinthians 15:17

The theories to explain away this historical event are as numerous as the theories to explain away the words of Jesus. First, let us examine the wrong tomb theory, which is simple in origin. Skeptics assert that Mary, Peter, and John all went to the wrong tomb on Sunday morning. Convincing? No. How can three people at three different times run to the wrong burial place of the man they greatly loved? Mary was first and reported back to the disciples. Then Peter and John left together but John out ran Peter and arrived first. Three separate people and all were mistaken, even after an extremely short period of just three days since the burial? Couldn't they have asked Joseph of Arimathea where his tomb was located if there was any doubt? Of course, if it was the wrong tomb, then Jesus' body was still dead in the right tomb. Why didn't the Romans and Jews ever produce this body when the resurrection story spread?

Second, the Swoon Theory, which as the wrong tomb theory, is simple in origin, too. Skeptics believe that Jesus was beaten mercilessly into a coma. The Roman executioner mistook his lifeless appearance as being dead. He was buried but at some point over the Sabbath holidays of Passover, he awoke from his comatose state, was physically revived and... pushed away a stone that ten men had to move. Then he wrestled and conquered two soldiers earnestly standing guard with their lives on the line, walked back to the hiding place of his disciples and convinced one and all, that he died and rose again without any need for medial attention. Objections are many! Medical experts and historical scholars agree, that any man who experienced the bodily trauma that Jesus faced, with the proven technique of Roman crucifixion, would have never survived such an ordeal. As Roman Law dictates, once a defendant is found guilty and is condemned to be crucified, the process must be overseen by a crucifixion specialist known as the Carnifix Serarum (literally, the "flesh nailer"). [10] The survival rate is zilch.

In addition, Jesus would have died again at some point, kept hidden and then buried again. At which point, his erroneous resurrection would have been exposed and his followers dispersed or recanting their faith to save their lives. None of which happened.

The final is the Hallucination theory. People only thought they had seen the risen Jesus but it was all an apparition. This is ridiculous. Hallucinations might happen to one person, at one time of distress and anxiety but the resurrection is something all together different. The risen Jesus was seen numerous times over a forty day period by over five hundred people. Mass hallucinations do not happen. If a mass hallucination was to occur over a massive amount of days, it would be a miracle! The same objections apply. Why didn't the Romans and Jews produce the corpse to shut down the false and fearlessly proclaimed message, that Christ was risen?

The only reasonable accusation is the Apostles purposely and knowingly lied about the resurrection, stole the body and beat the guards. This must be the best crisis management resolution in history. None of them expected his resurrection, as Scripture records, they went to the tomb with spices to anoint the dead body. Somehow these simple men, devised the most unbelievable story and lost their lives preaching a lie, while accumulating not fame and fortune, but persecution and prison.

Dinesh D'Souza: "We must ask whether these early Christians were serious about Christ's resurrection, whether they were being truthful about what they saw and whether it mattered to them. These questions are not difficult to answer. The disciples became so convinced of what they had seen that their dirges of lamentation were replaced with cries of joy. Proclaiming Christ crucified and Christ risen, they launched the greatest wave of religious conversion in history. The number of Christians increased from around one hundred at the time of Christ's death, to around thirty-million, by the early fourth century, when the Roman emperor, Constantine himself, converted to Christianity. These conversions occurred in the teeth of fierce opposition and the persecution of the greatest empire in the ancient world, the empire of Rome. The early Christians did not hesitate to identify themselves with a man who had been branded a traitor and a criminal. They endured imprisonment, torture, exile and death rather than renounce their commitment to a resurrected Christ. Even from a secular point of view, the evidence for the resurrection is surprisingly strong. Indeed, coming from so many witnesses with so much to lose, it might even be sufficient to convince an impartial jury in a court of law." [11]

Reality Known

Jesus is 100% man and 100% God. The secular arena will enthrone his human accomplishments and place of greatness in history. He is at minimum, a man most admired. Realistically, based on their assumption, Jesus cannot be God because god does not exist. Make him a reformer or a rabbi, a mystic or a mass deceiver but do not confess him as God. As comprehensively discussed in Chapter 3, God, through Jesus Christ, will individually save us as Christians believe or government through social engineering will collectively save us, as humanists, atheists, and statists believe. Personal salvation through Christ or collective liberation through government, what will America choose?

Section 3

The UnDivided

Chapter Nine

Foundation to the Consummation

If a house is divided against itself, that house cannot stand.
Mark 3:25

"Now, Lord, consider their threats and enable your servants to speak your word with great boldness. Stretch out your hand to heal and perform signs and wonders through the name of your holy servant Jesus." After they prayed, the place where they were meeting was shaken. And they were all filled with the Holy Spirit and spoke the word of God boldly. All the believers were one in heart and mind.
Acts 4:29-33

So Christ himself gave the apostles, the prophets, the evangelists, the pastors and teachers, to equip his people for works of service, so that the body of Christ may be built up until we all reach unity in the faith and in the knowledge of the Son of God and become mature, attaining to the whole measure of the fullness of Christ. Then we will no longer be infants, tossed back and forth by the waves, and blown here and there by every wind of teaching and by the cunning and craftiness of people in their deceitful scheming. Instead, speaking the truth in love, we will grow to become in every respect the mature body of him who is the head, that is, Christ. From him the whole body, joined and held together by every supporting ligament, grows and builds itself up in love, as each part does its work.
Ephesians 4:12-16

The summer of 2010 was a solemn year for Move the Earth. Constant personal financial lack had taken its toll. My family was, essentially, homeless as we slept on the concrete but carpeted basement floor of concerned and strapped family members. On April 10, I sowed our only substantial income, the Federal tax return, to pay the costs of a pro-life awareness and fundraising event which Move the Earth committed to in Paterson, NJ at Harvest Outreach Ministries. Broke and exhausted, I traveled south at 1a.m. down the tranquil section of the Garden State Parkway, past exit 120 and heading much further down the Jersey Shore. I asked the Lord, "Now what?" The reply was unusually quick and clear. "MTE's Jesus Shore, like MTV's Jersey Shore. Do a major Christian event in Seaside Heights, NJ and call it MTE's Jesus Shore." The next morning, I made my initial contact with a local church, shared the idea, and the process began. After many hurdles and roadblocks, the promise of God never failed. Media coverage loved the angle, hoping for controversy. There was none. It was not the intention. Critics and supporters from across the country had MTE's Jesus Shore on their lips, their blogs and their morning and evening news. After returning from discussing Jesus Shore on FOX and Friends, the #1 cable news morning show, I went back to the basement and laid on the floor to nap. The words would roll off my tongue with less effort and less expectancy, "Now what?" as my eyes grew heavy in the late morning rest.

Approximately three weeks later, the local pastors met for our weekly prayer. It was a thin crowd and over the coming months it would only get thinner. I closed my eyes, participated in prayer and then saw an image in my mind's eye of the body of Jesus on the cross. The reply of "Now what?" had come. "This is my body," the Lord said. Immediately it downloaded, whether in seconds or minutes, I do not know but it was again as before on the Parkway, quick and clear. Jesus compared His body during the Last Supper, to a crucified offering given for us.

> And he took bread, gave thanks and broke it, and gave it to
> them, saying, "This is my body given for you;
> do this in remembrance of me."
> **Luke 22:19**

The Body of Christ, spiritually, is on the earth through the Church. The Body of Christ, physically, was on the earth and hung on the cross, a point of reference per Jesus. That is when the image became intrinsically visible. Jesus showed me the history of His spiritual body on earth, through his physical body on the cross. Without researching any historical background, the 2,000 years of church history flooded my mind in conformity to Christ's crucified body. This was and this is, His body.

The following are the general main points concerning church history and how they relate to the Body of Christ.

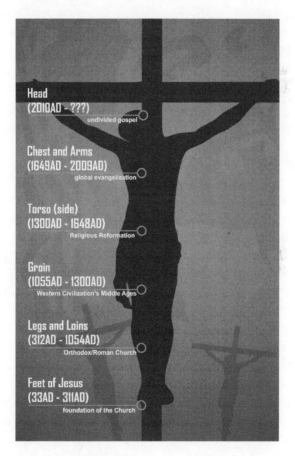

The Feet of Jesus (33AD-311AD) — The Foundation of the Church
This includes the times of the Apostles and the early church fathers, ending around the onset of the Constantine era, around the year 311AD. This was a time of great persecution, represented by the wounded, nail pierced feet and blood of Jesus. The two feet, pierced and overlapping as one, reveal the uniting of

Israel and the Gentiles at the beginning of the Church Age, known as a Jewish sect called, The Way. The Way soon became known as "Christians" upon spreading into the Gentile world.

The Legs of Jesus (312AD-1054AD) — Orthodox Church of the East and Roman Catholic Church of the West

This long period of close but separate theologies and traditions are represented by the length of Jesus' two legs (east and west) and includes the year 1000AD to the turn of a new millennium, which is the mid point of the Church Age. Soon thereafter, in the year 1054AD there was the "Great Schism" between the East and West Church, which correlates to the section of the body where the legs split from one torso into two limbs.

The Groin of Jesus (1055AD — 1300AD) — the place of intimacy and covering as part of Western Civilization's Middle Ages

This period of time was famous for the lack of education and progress that earlier periods and the later "Enlightenment" brought to civilization. Religious knowledge had a dim veil, as it was hidden from the common layman, being forbidden to be translated apart from Latin. The Monks and the Mystics, through their intimacy with the Lord, became the strength of the Church, in keeping the knowledge of the Word and the arts alive through this period.

The Torso of Jesus (1300AD-1648AD) — the split in Jesus' body represents the Religious Reformation

The inner discontent started in the bowels of the Body. The discontent was found in the early reformers from John Wycliffe and John Hus, in the 1300s to Martin Luther's Ninety-Five Thesis, in 1517. The Body "split" over the blood "grace" and the water "the word" that poured forth from Jesus' wound. The religious wars of Europe would unfortunately follow this split, culminating in the Thirty Years War, in 1648.

The Chest and Arms of Jesus (1649AD-2009AD) — various denomi-nations, great awakenings, revivals and the completion of global evangelization

After the Reformation wound, the Body became stronger (chest) and went in independent, theological directions, resulting in numerous denominations. These differences led the Body away from each other (arms pointing outward) but through this position, the Church reached the world over the next three centuries with missionaries, the first and second Great Awakenings and global expeditions. Different denominations (parts of the arms) helped to accomplish this mission — from Pentecostal outpourings, to Baptist and Methodist revivals in America, the Catholic Renewal and more.

The end of his arms signifies the completion. The gospel has gone out into all the world. This is represented by His hands which, as His feet, are pierced with blood flowing from his wounds. This accounts for the persecution that is currently taking place at the ends of the earth in nations such as Sudan, China, Pakistan, Saudi Arabia, Indonesia, and other Islamic Sharia Law nations.

The Head of Jesus (2010AD-???) the UNDIVIDED proclamation of the gospel and the UNDIVIDED persecution at the end of the Church Age

The mouth of Jesus represents the unified proclamation of the Gospel and the core beliefs of the Christian faith (covered in Section II). The head of Jesus, that endured the crown of thorns, represents the global persecution of the Church. Similar to his feet and hands, the points of blood symbolize the hatred and suffering experienced by true followers of Christ. The soon and sure persecution which will follow in the days ahead will be a direct assault from progressive and secular governments, rooted in Humanism and the anti-Christian agenda which challenges the authority of Jesus and His Kingdom. The King of the Jews had thorns implanted in his brow as a mockery of His Lordship. The Kingdoms of this world are in conflict with the Kingdom of God. The clash has been intensifying as of late but the animosity of man's reign towards God's authority has been present since Christ.

I encourage you to read, pray and meditate over this intriguing and interesting snapshot of the spiritual and physical Body of Christ. This book cannot do justice in covering the scope of church history, briefly mentioned, in this prophetic overview. I dare not try to bullet point each reformer, revival or global state of persecution. There are other authoritative books that thoroughly cover each topic in detail with many references and historical accuracy.

My responsibility, for which Jesus Christ chose to reveal this hidden mystery, was for three specific reasons:

- Urge the Body to unify publicly for our Core Beliefs and the gospel of Jesus Christ, as God's sovereign timetable for the last great unified proclamation is at hand.

- Warn the Body of the coming persecution from the anti-Christian dominant, sexually immoral, lawless spirit which is gaining momentum and power in our new secular, global world. (Chapter 10 — The Spirit of Lawlessness)

- Alert the Body to the urgency of the hour. The days are short. The task is great. The time is now. Christ is watching and Christ is coming! (Chapter 11 — The Urgency of the Hour)

I will now finish this specific chapter under the banner of unity and my hardline rejection of ecumenicalism. In my prompting of unity, I must balance such an overdone message with needed instruction on real reasons to be cautious of unity.

The campaign message, "We Stand — UNDIVIDED," at its very core, communicates strength, purpose and opposition.

The word "stand" has a connotation of alertness, readiness, and confidence.

As the Church, we are standing for something and someone. Of course, the law of logic will reply, if you are standing for, then there is something or someone who is standing against. Millennial Christians have a hard time admitting the unavoidable. No matter how many women the faith community rescues from human trafficking or the number of clean water wells we build with our resources, the spirit of the world will continue to hate and oppose our faith and our Christ.

It is often understood that the Millennial Generation is 'cause' oriented. Yet, Christ is not a cause but a person. It is easier and more self-satisfying to serve a cause than to submit to an authority. A 'cause' offers a common goal, while Christ offers repentance, responsibility and eternal rewards. The abolition of evil is the kingdom, and our social justice advocates are pursuing it without the king!

John the Apostle, often referred to as the Apostle of Love because of his repetitive usage of the word *love* in referring to God's nature and Christ's mission, balanced his message with the Greek word *kosmos*, or world. For instance, *kosmos* or the world's system was used 103 times in John's gospel and epistles. The word love was

> The word "stand" has a connotation of alertness, readiness, and confidence.

used 104 times. No one spoke more often or more clearly than John about God's love and the world's system that opposed it. The classic and well respected *Strong Concordance* accurately points out that, specifically in John, the *kosmos* or world's system, is opposed to God. Ultimately, a God who created the world, loved the world to such an extent that He would enter the world to save it. Yet, the world did not recognize him or receive him but instead, hated Him without a cause.

King Jesus perfectly showered the world with His Father's love and grace. Despite his track record of good, he was hated and betrayed by the masses for His claims of divinity. The Pharisees never approved His message but to be fair, everyone by Holy Week's end was against his message. Good works did not improve his public approval rating.

> "We are not stoning you for any good work," they replied,
> "but for blasphemy, because you,
> a mere man, claim to be God."
> **John 10:33**

I share this verse to remind the popularity seeking Church that we will never be late night celebrities or celebrated political personalities. We are not of this world. We were, but we were called out and responded to the master's merciful and meek voice. If the world hated Christ, it will hate us.

Shockingly, this view of opposition was the compelling narrative that Jesus used to command unity among his true followers. Their message was to burst onto the scene in a pre-Christianized world and they desperately needed one another. In similar fashion, we are living in a post-Christian America and we need one another. Jesus told us to 'love one another...because the world will hate you.'

> This is my command: Love each other. If the world hates you, keep in mind that it hated me first. If you belonged to the world, it would love you as its own. As it is, you do not belong to the world, but I have chosen you out of the world. That is why the world hates you. Remember what I told you: 'A servant is not greater than his master.' If they persecuted me, they will persecute you also. If they obeyed my teaching, they will obey yours also. They will treat you this way because of my name, for they do not know the one who sent me. If I had not come and spoken to them, they would not be guilty of sin; but now they have no excuse for their sin. Whoever hates me hates my Father as well. If I had not done among them the works no one else did, they would not be guilty of sin. As it is, they have seen, and yet they have hated both me and my Father. But this is to fulfill what is written in their Law: 'They hated me without reason.'
> **John 15:17-25**

John 14-17 is the longest, recorded, word for word conversation Jesus had with his disciples in private and the longest, recorded, word for word prayer Jesus had with his Father. The full content of his departing monologue was such: I am the Vine and you need to be connected to me. You are the branches and will grow and extend in different directions but you have the same life source. The *kosmos*, the world's system will oppose you and hate you, so my command is to love one another. His intercessory prayer over the future of his Church in John 17 was strikingly similar. In essence, the world is going to oppose them but I want the world to believe in them. Father, help them to be one. To further compliment this strategy of spirit empowered oneness in the face of opposition, the Apostle Paul, wisely used the same fact for the precise purpose of unity.

> ...stand firm in the one Spirit, striving together as one for the faith of the gospel without being frightened in any way by those who oppose you.
> **Philippians 1:27-28**

Against Christ and His Church are forces, figures and finances which seemingly work independently as the world turns. However, this anti-Christian contingency is unified spiritually through the deceptive hands of the devil. Different platforms, different causes but the same core plan. Shame, scorn and silence the Christian voice.

The temptation to tamper the more challenging messages of scripture, to avoid the plot of an outcast, is appealing.

Here is the unmentioned truth. The contemporary Church prefers to soften the teachings of Jesus regarding sexual morality, holiness, purity and his claim to being the exclusive path of salvation; indirectly labeling other faiths as false prophets. Why? The Christian wants to be accepted. George Whitfield, the British evangelist who helped spark the first Great Awakening, held a polar opposite view of the Christian experience and acceptance in society when he said, "If you are going to walk with Jesus Christ, you are going to be opposed.... In our days, to be a true Christian is really to become a scandal."

A post resurrection Jesus was never trendy or well-liked. The Church reads the gospels through New Testament eyes when it, in fact, records the end of the Old Testament. Jesus soared in popularity during his earthly ministry because it was a Messianic Age in Israel. The people were itching for the Kingdom of God, oppressed by Roman rule and mistrustful of their spiritual leaders. The fanfare of Christ and the swell of support came from the undercurrent of a revolution. His disciples, along with the masses, waited and anticipated that the Kingdom would come. Jesus of Nazareth was the Messiah. The disappointment and deception around Passover crushed their hopes. Jesus claimed to be God; blasphemy! The old was passing away and the new was beginning — crucify! The Prince of the Air, Satan would have his hour and face his judgement. The anti-Christian spirit was loosed upon the earth. The blood of the saints cry out around the throne to this day. Clearly, a fashionable faith is not feasible.

Against Christ and His Church are forces, figures and finances which seemingly work independently as the world turns. However, this anti-Christian contingency is unified spiritually through the deceptive hands of the devil. Different platforms, different causes but the same core plan. Shame, scorn and silence the Christian voice.

"I am sending you out like sheep among wolves.
Therefore be as shrewd as snakes and as innocent as doves."
Matthew 10:16

The spirit of the world understands the power of mass numbers. From the Conservative TEA Party movement, to the Arab Spring across the Middle East, there is undeniable and unstoppable power in agreement; the fall of the Berlin Wall on one side of history and the Bolshevik Revolution on the other side; from the crowd laying palm branches at Jesus' feet on Palm Sunday, to the crowd watching in pleasurable horror as those feet are pierced on Good Friday. The Church needs bold, mass numbers of people to cause change for Christ.

Boards of Directors do not have to agree on all business decisions but they must agree on the mission and purpose of the organization. Husbands and wives do not agree on every household decision but they must agree to remain faithful to their covenantal marriage vows. Political groups viscously barrage their own party during primaries then 'fall in line' during, the more important, general election. The Church needs to reach beyond our differences to keep the determined course of the organization, family and institution.

If we fail in this hour of unprecedented opportunity and hostility, to join as one voice in the undivided, global proclamation of the gospel, we will still accompany one another to our court appearances for violating speech laws or personal and corporate bankruptcy hearings. Before long, congregation members will lose their liberty and employment status due to their refusal to deny the scriptures in the area of sexual misconduct. The Church will lose the tax exempt status within years.

Yes, we are standing for Christ and the Core Beliefs. Shamefully, others are standing against Christ and our Core Beliefs. Beloved, we must replant our feet firmly in the ground and stand.

Therefore put on the full armor of God, so that when the day
of evil comes, you may be able to stand your ground, and after
you have done everything, to stand. Stand firm then...
Ephesians 6:13-14

Unlike an interfaith, ecumenical memorial service where poems replace the prophets and choirs attempt to comfort and not convict our souls, UNDIVIDED stands to contend for our faith, not compromise our faith. Whether in controversy or convenience, the Church stands convinced of absolute, revealed truth. In plain English, we are standing firm and holding our ground on the same side. The world is changing but, as unearthly pilgrims, we refuse to change with it.

The CIA and the FBI did not collaborate often before 9/11, then reality unleashed our common foe. The consensus to partner in the war against terrorism superseded distrust and competition. We are living in a post-9/11 world and we are living in a post-Christian world.

Unity is not about forming an expansive, all-inclusive church doctrine or organization. For this very reason, Protestants left the Catholic Church. Reformers did not agree with Canon Law or the authority of the Pope and the institutional hierarchy. We need, and I support, the ability to follow conscience. Individuality and the priesthood of the believer should be revered. Moreover, we need to celebrate the diversity which God has made in one body. The underlying theme is for us to stand in this hour, and how can a house which is divided... stand?

Surprisingly, Jesus' prayer for unity in John 17 is not the foundational biblical scripture I will rely upon to build my argument for individual diversity and collective unity. Instead, I inject the very nature of God.

> Hear, O Israel: The Lord our God, the Lord is one.
> **Deuteronomy 6:4**

The Lord is 'echad,' a Hebrew word used, most often, as a unified one and sometimes as numeric oneness. For example, when God said in Genesis 2:24, "the two shall become one [echad] flesh" it is the same word for "one" that was used in Deut 6:4. Male and female are numerically two as singles, with two distinct personalities. Dr. Michael Brown says, "Even if we follow the common rendering, 'Hear Oh Israel; the Lord our God, the Lord is one.' It's important to understand that the word, Echad, does not point to absolute unity, it simply means one, as in one day consisting of night and day, Genesis 1:5 and a man and woman coming together to become one, Genesis 2:24." [1]

Furthermore, Dr. Brown explains the express difference of the other 'one' in Hebrew, the word 'yachid.' The debate over the implications of the various usages of two Hebrew words [Yachid vs. Echad] translated "one" is as intriguing as it is complex. The etymology of the Hebrew word *yachid* (one) is derived from *echad* in the same way that the English word "only" is derived from the word "one". That *yachid* is from the same root family of words as *echad* is seen from the similarity of spelling. So "*yachid*" is to "only," as "*echad*" is to "one." [2] "This is most troubling for Anti-Trinitarians since the word *yachid*, the main Hebrew word for solitary oneness, is never used in reference to God." [3]

Forgive the theological high ground but my eyes are open to the awesomeness of God's triune oneness and to the fact that the Church, as the Body of Jesus Christ, who is God-incarnate, can walk 'in Christ' as individuals who supernaturally are one (*echad*).

In Christ makes it possible. The mind of Christ makes it practical. The timeline of the Church Age places us in the head of Christ. The distinct location for an undivided proclamation, followed by the undivided persecution. In the head of Christ, is the mind of Christ. To successfully proclaim the faith in this new century, we must humble ourselves, and refrain from provoking one another. In context, Paul was instructing the church of Philippi to be united in Christ to stay strong against those who would oppose them (Philippians chapter 1).

> Therefore if you have any encouragement from being united with Christ, if any comfort from his love, if any common sharing in the Spirit, if any tenderness and compassion, then make my joy complete by being like-minded, having the same love, being one in spirit and of one mind. Do nothing out of selfish ambition or vain conceit. Rather, in humility value others above yourselves, not looking to your own interests but each of you to the interests of the others. In your relationships with one another, have the same mindset as Christ Jesus: Who, being in very nature God, did not consider equality with God something to be used to his own advantage; rather, he made himself nothing by taking the very nature of a servant, being made in human likeness. And being found in appearance as a man, he humbled himself by becoming obedient to death—even death on a cross!
> **Philippians 2:1-8**

May the God who gives endurance and encouragement give you
the same attitude of mind toward each other that Christ Jesus
had, so that with one mind and one voice you may glorify the
God and Father of our Lord Jesus Christ. Accept one another,
then, just as Christ accepted you, in order to bring praise to God.
Romans 15:5-7

...we have the mind of Christ.
1 Corinthians 2:16

In context, Paul instructs the Philippi, Roman and young, carnal
Corinthian churches to stop their divisions and worldly jealously for
the mind of Christ does not think and interpret relationships in that
fashion. Christ puts others above himself; serving other's needs rather
than being served.

Paul gives us further practical living points in putting others
above yourself as the mind of Christ would do.

Though I am free and belong to no one, I have made myself
a slave to everyone, to win as many as possible. To the Jews I
became like a Jew, to win the Jews. To those under the law I
became like one under the law (though I myself am not under
the law), so as to win those under the law. To those not having
the law I became like one not having the law (though I am not
free from God's law but am under Christ's law), so as to win
those not having the law. To the weak I became weak, to win
the weak. I have become all things to all people so that by all
possible means I might save some. I do all this for the sake of
the gospel, that I may share in its blessings.
1 Corinthians 9:19-23

Hermeneutically applying this verse in an unwise manner, some
believers have compromised their faith and lifestyle to please others
and become more relatable. Again, in context, Paul is comparing his
leadership and rights of an apostle to his humble servanthood. He could
demand that others become like him, as he rightfully is an exceptional,
admired apostle, worthy of respect and honor. Instead, he thought less
of himself.

For by the grace given me I say to every one of you: Do not
think of yourself more highly than you ought, but rather think
of yourself with sober judgment, in accordance with the faith
God has distributed to each of you. For just as each of us has
one body with many members, and these members do not all
have the same function, so in Christ we, though many, form
one body, and each member belongs to all the others. We
have different gifts, according to the grace given to each of
us. If your gift is prophesying, then prophesy in accordance
with your faith; if it is serving, then serve; if it is teaching, then
teach; if it is to encourage, then give encouragement; if it is
giving, then give generously; if it is to lead, do it diligently; if it
is to show mercy, do it cheerfully.

Romans 12:3-8

Pastors regularly teach this principle for church members and
volunteers. How easily it is overlooked when applied to local pastors
and the specific vision and ministry God has assigned them to do.
Churches differ in strengths and weaknesses, outreach programs, worship style and personalities of leadership which connect with different
types of attendees, all within the framework and oversight of Christ
Himself.

Love, the greatest of all, is the minimum and maximum of what is
needed. All we need is love. Love for God's people displaces knowledge
as the nucleus of our faith.

For a preacher who stresses and emphasizes core beliefs and
warns of subtle deception, I do not take my statement lightly. Knowledge is the gift that God has given us to know Him and the world
around us. Love is the gift that God has given us to be like Him — in
the world around us. Back to the Corinthian church:

Now about food sacrificed to idols:
We know that "We all possess knowledge."
But knowledge puffs up while love builds up. Those who think
they know something do not yet know as they ought to know.
But whoever loves God is known by God.

1 Corinthians 8:1-3

Knowledge is not as important as loving your brother or fellow pastor. Grievously, the Church has judged 'who is our brother' not by the love they have for the biblical Jesus but

Love, the greatest of all, is the minimum and maximum of what is needed. All we need is love. Love for God's people displaces knowledge as the nucleus of our faith.

for the right knowledge interpreted through our traditional lens. Keep in mind, this division of knowledge has separated the Body, making our ability to stand against Christ's true enemies increasingly difficult.

Knowledge is always incomplete and imperfect in this life. We see dimly, while judging strictly.

Paul encouraged the more mature believers to consider the faith of their weaker brother when in public. In the same way, the denominational Church should remain consistent and faithful in their statement of beliefs according to conscience in private gatherings but our love for our fellow brother should trump our preferences. We should, instead prefer our brother above ourselves in public assemblies and corporate worship services.

If I speak in the tongues of men or of angels, but do not have
love, I am only a resounding gong or a clanging cymbal. If I
have the gift of prophecy and can fathom all mysteries and all
knowledge, and if I have a faith that can move mountains, but
do not have love, I am nothing. If I give all I possess to the poor
and give over my body to hardship that I may boast,
but do not have love, I gain nothing.
1 Corinthians 13:1-3

Doctrine and demonstration will pass away but love will remain. To the conservative believer-if your theology limits your ability to speak in tongues, as your conscience and understanding teaches the gifts have ceased, then continue to speak in the tongues of men. However, if you are unable to accept and love your brother, who through conscience and understanding believes he is speaking in the tongues of angels, then your tongue and your knowledge has hindered your true calling to love. To the Pentecostal believer, on the other hand-you must also accept and love the conservative brother who desires your fellowship without your insistence that, 'tongues is for today.' Praying in the tongues of men or the tongues of angels is not the spiritual

> Knowledge is always incomplete and imperfect in this life. We see dimly, while judging strictly.

measuring rod of a biblically accurate and acceptable prayer. That stick is much shorter and carries much more weight.

> In that day you will no longer ask me anything.
> Very truly I tell you, my Father will give you
> whatever you ask in my name. Until now you have not asked for
> anything in my name. Ask and you will receive,
> and your joy will be complete.
> **John 16:23-24**

Citing the complexities of the Corinthian Church and Paul's correction concerning division caused by pride and knowledge, I shared valuable, practical, godly steps for ministers to consider in standing and serving together with co-laborers, pastors of like faith but not necessarily identical faith. God does not want us to have the same mind, but Christ's mind. He wants us to be lovers of others who prefer our separate but equal pastors above ourselves. As a leader in building lasting ties with area pastors, I know it is easier to walk in relationships together when you are weeping for revival. If we can solidify our core foundational beliefs and reset our focal point on the end goal, preaching the gospel and preparing the way of the Lord, the rest will come together for God's glory, through His sovereignty, in our local churches and denominations.

In theory, I offer nothing new. In practice, I offer something proven. Love those who love the Godhead differently than me. As a father, all my children relate to me differently. Some are loud and touchy, and others introverted. My love is unconditional and their expression of their personal love for me is equivalent to the other but not the same.

Moving on from lessons learned in the Corinthian Church, let us delve into the book of Acts, specifically chapter 15. Three main obstacles hindering solitary and agreement surfaced in the early church and effect us today: Religion, Race, Relationships.

Religion

Acts 15 is our earliest glimpse of humanity struggling to govern the Church. As usual, there is division over religion (Law of Moses applicable to Gentiles), division over race (Gentiles, coheirs with Israel in Christ), and division over relationships (Long time friends Paul and Barnabas have a moment of 'intense fellowship' over John Mark). Here is *Matthew Henry's Commentary*, "In this chapter we find the apostles had other work cut out for them that was not so pleasant. The Christians and ministers were engaged in controversy. When they should have been making war on the Devil's Kingdom, they had much to do to keep peace in Christ's kingdom."[4] Nearly 2,000 years later and our attitudes and differences continue to hinder our collective influence. Instead of promoting our Core Beliefs which are dwindling away, the Church is fractured over lesser known biblical interpretations. Historically, the Church would unify and rally for social issues such as abortion and marriage or for social causes as poverty, drug epidemics or human trafficking. I support and admire both unified fronts. However, these are secondary causes for unity. The primary cause for unity is our common faith, which produces our moral reasoning and our compassionate works. I suppose it is needless to repeat Section II.

Our faith is under fire by secularists to undo religion and undermine morality.

The enemies of the gospel, often mentioned or referenced in this book, are not questioning our doctrinal differences as water baptism, pre destination, church government, John MacAuthor's *Strange Fire* or Michael Brown's *Authentic Fire*. Shrewdly, they are resolute in their objective to eradicate the essential core beliefs which blanket nearly every church website across denominational and non-denominational backgrounds. Need I repeat — God is the Creator, Jesus is the Savior, the Bible is true, the Devil is real, and we are saved by grace.

I am not implying our theological differences are not important and worthy of discussion but unworthy of division. Surely, proper exegetical research and proper application is paramount.

> Our faith is under fire by secularists to undo religion and undermine morality.

Above all, Christianity is well-known for theologians and the study of knowing God. The imperative of the Christian experience is to know God, not only intellectually but intimately.

D'Souza explains the difference in the monotheistic faiths. "Judaism and Islam are primarily religions of law; there is a divine lawgiver who issues edicts that are authoritative both for nature and for human beings. Christianity, by contrast, is not a religion of law but a religion of creed. Christianity has always been obsessed with doctrine, which is thought to be a set of true beliefs about man's relationship with God." [5]

Do not assume that I am soft on doctrine or my charismatic leanings take doctrinal issues less serious. I do not hop from mountain top to mountain top in my experiences with God. I am an intellectual introvert; conservative in my personality and emotional comfort zones.

It is because I take the seriousness of knowing God through His word that I believe the Church is obligated to advocate for our cherished common faith as one body.

I am not persuading the Church to bolster the number of miracles or water baptisms. I insist we stand undivided for the Christian faith and the knowledge of God, not collapse because of it.

As a bridge from religious to racial differences, the one experience that solidified the Church and was perceived as divine evidence of Israel's God accepting the pagan Gentiles was the baptism of the Holy Spirit, including speaking in tongues at the house of Cornelius in Acts 10. Ironically, what God sovereignly used to unite the Church, many are using to divide the Church. Our subjective experiences or non-experiences should not overrule our shared objective truth of sacred scripture.

Race

Moving on to race relations, though multicultural churches are thriving, Sunday morning remains separated by communities, albeit not segregated by choice. Since the majority of worshippers will attend a church that is within their community, social and economical factors contribute to the distinguishable racial separation within the Body of Christ. Above all, politics has created a great divide and suspicion among spiritual leaders, community organizers, and church organizations.

The charismatic branch of Christianity has recently focused on making amends with the stains of racial prejudice in the past. In November 2013, the executive leadership of the Assemblies of God hosted the executive leadership of the Church of God in Christ who represent over six million members. Ann Carol, from *Charisma Magazine* reported, "The historic meeting marks the first time the full leadership of these Pentecostal movements—two of the largest in the US—have gathered specifically to dialogue together." [6]

The Empowered21 global prayer initiative has garnished a wide range

> It is because I take the seriousness of knowing God through His word that I believe the Church is obligated to advocate for our cherished common faith as one body.

of diverse support that extends beyond cultural, racial issues to unite nations. "I see Empowered 21 as the Body coming together again. So important. So necessary," Dr. Paul Dhinakaran predicted. "When brothers dwell together in unity, the Lord commands a blessing." [7]

If the Cross is the work of God that reconciled the Jew and Gentile as one body, can it not also be the platform of faith that can reconcile the manifold parts of the Christian Church?

> For he himself is our peace, who has made the two groups
> one and has destroyed the barrier, the dividing wall of hostility,
> by setting aside in his flesh the law with its commands and
> regulations.His purpose was to create in himself one new
> humanity out of the two, thus making peace, and in one body
> to reconcile both of them to God through the cross, by which
> he put to death their hostility. He came and preached peace to
> you who were far away and peace to those who were near. For
> through him we both have access to the Father by one Spirit.
> **Ephesians 2:14-18**

Relationships

Religion and race are barriers to official, recognizable, national and international Christian unity. The real problem that negatively effects the influence of the Kingdom of God at the local community level are the broken and offended relationships between pastors who are serving Christ in the same area. These co-laborers, with their authentic natural leadership qualities, have a difficult time serving and submitting 'one to another.' As stated unapologetically earlier, men of God would do well to remember the mind of Christ in managing their relationships.

Jesus had to resolve feelings of rejection, mistrust and doubt among his disciples following his resurrection. Relationships were imploding while Pentecostal power was weeks away from exploding. Peter felt rejected, as he self-condemned himself for rejecting Christ. He needed restoration and reassurance in the presence of his peers. Others must have had a sense of mistrust due to Judas' betrayal. Would another disciple fold under pressure and tell the Roman authorities where they were hiding? Thomas doubted the resurrection because he was absent when Jesus visited the group. Today, pastors feel rejected when other local pastors and churches do not attend invited meetings or events. Pastors guard themselves against trusting relationships due to church splits and failed partnerships with other ministers. Finally, the attitude of God must move in my church or He is not moving at all outlook that Thomas had holds back mountain moving faith in corporate prayer, and leads to jealousy and criticism towards the success of other ministries. Christ had to remove these roadblocks to revival.

The success to navigate through issues of religion, race and relationships in the early church, should encourage us. Jew and Gentile, Paul and Barnabas, Cessationists and Continuationists are two but one. The Godhead is three but one.

I am optimistic as I observe the recent standpoint of major Christian leaders. Pope Francis has gone on record stating the devil is keeping Catholics and Evangelicals 'divided,' as he persecutes the entire Church. [8] The Southern Baptist Convention amended their policy regarding Charismatic missionaries. [9] Bishop T.D. Jakes, Bishop Harry Jackson and James Robison launched the Reconciled Church to promote racial healing. [10] God is restructuring His Church for the 21st century. The outdated ineffective divisions are now adjusting to a clear vision forward. The Church must stand UNDIVIDED to not only endure but overcome in the years ahead.

The Church would profit from an independent but dependent mentality. This is often the basis for archaic covenants and current international treaties. The old fashioned way of thinking strategically when faced with hardships and tough odds was to make a covenant, a deal, an agreement between two parties which would benefit both. Uncertainty and fear have shown to be faithful motivators in joining separate powers to find shared strength as a means of mutual survival, which outweighed the adverse outcome of autonomous annihilation.

In August of 1941, a secret meeting took place at sea between President Franklin Roosevelt and British Prime Minister Winston Churchill. These two men met to discuss the German Nazi advancement threatening Europe. This war time necessity was the first of its kind between these two political behemoths. The United States preferred to restrain itself from over involvement in a war that did not directly affect them. However, Churchill was convincing that the Americans and English had a common brotherhood. The language, the Christian faith and the shared history of their people groups made their sovereign nations interconnected. To further his case, German speaking Hitler was an enemy of the English people, culture and law. The Trans-Atlantic Treaty was signed. America guaranteed to stand with the British in defeating the invading Nazi regime.

What led these two men who never shook hands before to pledge their people, their economies and stake their nation's future with their do or die commitment for each other's national benefit? A recognizable and definable common foundation, the English language, history and a common enemy, the socialist despot Adolf Hitler, convinced them to partner as allies.

As Roosevelt and Churchill before us, the Church has a common foundation, a common faith, a common future, a common enemy and a common end. Built upon Christ our cornerstone, our foundation and faith is inseparable. Targeted by our mutual enemy, our unmistakable and linked future must be faced with courage and commitment. Unity is not only a beautiful thing. It is a necessary thing.

> How good and pleasant it is when God's people
> live together in unity!
> It is like precious oil poured on the head,
> running down on the beard,
> running down on Aaron's beard,
> down on the collar of his robe.
> **Psalm 133:1-2**

This verse sums up the cost of standing UNDIVIDED that few are willing to pay. Unity is as precious oil. The ointment was extracted by first crushing the fruit and then pressing the crushed mass. So it is and so it must be. The Bride, unapologetically holding fast to the faith despite the vehement hatred of those who oppose Christ and His kingdom, will face an unheard amount of pressure to forfeit the faith in the days ahead. The milquetoast emerging evangelical or liberal denomination clergy member may bypass such a tragic end. For us, the UNDIVIDED, we will not run dry of oil as the five virgins did in Matthew 25. Our lamps will unceasingly shine. The suffering and intolerance which is on the horizon towards Christ's Church will be the unifying factor. The more we are pressed and persecuted, the more precious oil we produce. Unity is pleasant but the process is tremendously painful.

Chapter Ten

The Spirit of Lawlessness

Concerning the coming of our Lord Jesus Christ and our being
gathered to him, we ask you, brothers and sisters, not to
become easily unsettled or alarmed by the teaching allegedly
from us—whether by a prophecy or by word of mouth or by
letter—asserting that the day of the Lord has already come.
Don't let anyone deceive you in any way, for that day will not
come until the rebellion occurs and the man of lawlessness is
revealed, the man doomed to destruction....
For the secret power of lawlessness is already at work;
but the one who now holds it back will continue to do so
till he is taken out of the way.
Thessalonians 2:1-3, 7

He will speak against the Most High and oppress his holy
people and try to change the set times and the laws.
Daniel 7:25

Therefore, dear friends, since you have been forewarned,
be on your guard so that you may not be carried away by the
error of the lawless and fall from your secure position.
But grow in the grace and knowledge of our
Lord and Savior Jesus Christ.
To him be glory both now and forever! Amen.
2 Peter 3:17-18

Telemachus contemplated the gross sins and godlessness of his known world. It is fair to say, he was grieved by the violent blood culture which made his normal life seem not normal. The Roman gluttony of sexual orgies and gory gladiator games were enough to keep him far removed from the center of Gentile debauchery and content at home in Asia. The mainstream opinion which chattered in the marketplaces approved the conventional lifestyles and love feasts. To them, it was common, it was acceptable but to Telemachus, it was not right.

As Todd Starnes, author and FOX news contributor, says, "I am a Duck Dynasty guy, living in a Miley Cyrus world." [1] The Asian monk Telemachus was a man of prayer and fasting, living in a seductive and brutal world. In the fourth century, this humble rural devotee from a remote village believed he heard the voice of God clearly say, "Go to Rome." He would travel for weeks on foot across the tough terrain until he reached his destination, the city of Rome. The best of us would have probably never left, let alone complete the task which was laid before him. He sacrificed his energy, time and resources in his "out of your mind" Spirit-led journey of faith. Another sacrifice which would forever change an empire would soon be required.

At the time of his arrival, the city was celebrating a triumph over the defeat of the Goths. Part of this festive atmosphere included the famous and infamous gladiator games at the awe-inspiring Coliseum. The crowds were massive and energetic. This quiet monk was, visibly, a newbie in town. I can only imagine how nervous and intimidated he felt. His eyes might have been following the crowds into the arena but his feet were being directed by the Lord.

Once inside the arena, he saw the gladiators approach one another and then swiftly turn to face the Emperor. "We who are about to die salute you," bravely pledged the insane men. Telemachus heard of such murderous games back at the faraway settlement he called home. Now, it was different. Out of sight, out of mind, ignorance is bliss for the blind man. He was now sovereignly led to stand in the midst of unrestrained barbarity. The thrill of the crowd was tangible. Adrenaline and testosterone oozed from pores already saturated with strong drink. His eyes froze, tunnel vision on the gladiators, then slowly rotating to the crowd, over to the Emperor, hesitantly back to the gladiators. The situation intensified in slow motion. The stomping of feet shook the tier he stood on. He knew these men were about to die just to honor the Emperor and please the crowd. Entertainers, addicted to adoration, do the most unpleasant and shocking acts to stay relevant.

Telemachus was burdened. Men, made in the image of God, men, who Christ Jesus died for, men, controlled by the sinful nature which Telemachus himself struggled against; these men were losing their lives while senators and slave traders talked business and politics with little care or concern for the consequences.

From out of his belly, he whispered these words, "In the name of Christ, stop!" Slowly he felt a heavy grief come all over him. He began to speak these words with the heart of God. He randomly grabbed spectators and pleaded with them, "In the name of Christ, stop!" It was to no avail.

He pushed his way through the throng of attendees to finally reach the wall that separated the crowd from the arena floor. The wall was more of a perimeter than a boundary. No one would dare enter the gladiator arena until Telemachus did the unthinkable. He stepped over the wall and dropped to the floor. Weeping prophets do the most unpredictable and shocking acts in their worship of the Lord.

This scrawny Asian monk, just weeks before, was picking vegetables and serving the poor. He preferred the quiet life, void of controversy and conflict. God understood the spiritual struggle of good and evil, light and darkness, sin and righteousness. Telemachus had a new mission that he did not request but he was responsible to fulfill.

He slowly approached the larger gladiator, "In the name of Christ, stop!" The unexpected visitor caught the fighter off guard. Then Telemachus spread his hands towards the multitude, "In the name of Christ, stop!" He then turned his attention to the Emperor himself. Under the anointing and hand of God, he called for mercy upon the gladiators as he challenged and commanded the Emperor, "In the name of Christ, stop!" Without warning, the gladiator he was trying to save, took his spear and impaled Telemachus. His last words, according to Church history, "In the name of Christ, stop!"

His intentions were pure, humble, merciful but the culture hated the message. Their rage ravaged the monk. His body laid on the ground but his words sat heavy in their hearts. Silence hovered over the arena. The Holy Spirit was on the scene, doing ministry as only He can do. A reflective stillness arrested the masses. An innocent man who meant no harm suffered at the hands of their demonic desires. Spiritually blind eyes were softly opened. Everyone exited the Coliseum without saying a word. So moved by the sacrifice, Emperor Honorius issued a decree to cease all future Gladiator games.

An unpopular message polarized an otherwise pluralistic society.

The gladiators and the government benefited from the economic boost the lust of the flesh, the lust of the eyes, and the pride of life generated for the city. The meekness of a martyr humbled the glorious empire of Rome. One man, willing to receive the brunt of retribution and retaliation, stepped out of his comfort zone and into the cultural war zone. The Kingdom of God or God's dominion, was to reign over all creation.

The problem then, as it is now, the creation resists the Lordship of Jesus Christ. Their reception or rejection of his Lordship does not change the fact that he is Lord.

> Therefore God exalted him to the highest place and gave him
> the name that is above every name, that at the name of Jesus
> every knee should bow, in heaven and on earth and under the
> earth, and every tongue acknowledge that Jesus Christ is Lord,
> to the glory of God the Father.
> **Philippians 2:9-11**

The Telemachus story is rooted in Church history. There are disputes over the cause of his death. Some, as I described, mention the gladiator spearing him. Other accounts report the crowd stoning him to death. Either way, the moral application of the story does not change. The cause of Christ requires sacrifice and obedience, especially in a hostile world under the spiritual dominion of Satan.

There is a spirit that has been in the world since the dawn of rebellion, more clearly manifested after the first coming of Jesus Christ. It is anti-Christian and lawless.

> This is how you can recognize the Spirit of God: Every spirit
> that acknowledges that Jesus Christ has come in the flesh is
> from God, but every spirit that does not acknowledge Jesus is
> not from God. This is the spirit of the antichrist, which you have
> heard is coming and even now is already in the world. You, dear

children, are from God and have overcome them, because the
one who is in you is greater than the one who is in the world.
1 John 4:1-4

The Apostle John teaches us that the sprit of anti-christ is already in the world, but that we, The Church, have greater power to
overcome. The header of this chapter reminded us that the spirit of
lawlessness is already at work but that the power of Christ, through
his Church, is holding it back (2 Thess 2:7) until the time the saints
are 'caught up.' If you are not actively restraining the lawless spirit,
then you are not faithfully fulfilling your moral responsibility and basic Christian duty.

The image of Jesus on the cross in correlation with the history of
the Church age is astonishing. We are uniting in Christ — the head, one
Lord, one faith, one bap-
tism (Ephesians 4:5). The
end of the age of grace is
approaching. The coming
of the Lord is near! The

An unpopular message polarized an otherwise pluralistic society.

great UNDIVIDED proclamation of Christ is now, as represented by the
Mouth of Christ. The dreaded, UNDIVIDED persecution of the Church
is forthcoming, represented by the Brow of Christ that suffered the
thorns.

Eschatology experts focus heavily on observable events that signal the nearing of Christ's return. It is outside the scope of this book to
cover these prophetic events in detail. I want to draw attention to the
spirit in the world, so vividly described in the Scriptures, that would
increase in fury during the days preceding the coming of the Lord —
the spirit of lawlessness and the spirit of Anti-Christ.

To properly understand the job description of these two sinister
spirits, we must simplify their adjectives. The spirit is the noun; lawlessness and anti-christ are the adjectives. The word translated lawless
comes from the Greek word *anomia* or *anomos* — both meaning a lawless deed in the sense of having no law or not regarding the law. Anti-
Christ is translated almost directly from the Greek word *antichristos* or
against the Christ. In total, these two unified spirits are preparing the
way for the Man of Lawlessness, often described by the apocalyptic
term, the Anti-Christ.

Please do not squirm in your seat and disengage from the message. No one knows who this man is, when he will publicly make himself known, or if he is even alive. Some scholars do not interpret Revelation as describing a single world ruler who will oppose Christ but a Beast system of government, economy, religion, and military.

I am not obsessed with the study of last days but I will uncover the spirit of this age that is prepping the hearts and minds of people to easily and willingly embrace the world community which humanists, atheists, and statists are tirelessly trying to form. As previously mentioned throughout this book, the objects of resistance are moral laws and the Christian Faith. The spirit of lawlessness is assigned to change or ignore the laws, the spirit of anti-christ is assigned to vilify and cause mass hatred towards Christ's Church.

Silence the Church, remove moral restraints and it's a near turnkey operation for world dominance.

Be encouraged, Telemachus and others from heaven's Hall of Faith in Hebrews 11, have paid the ultimate sacrifice without regret.

> Therefore, since we are surrounded by such a great cloud of witnesses, let us throw off everything that hinders and the sin that so easily entangles. And let us run with perseverance the race marked out for us, fixing our eyes on Jesus, the pioneer and perfecter of faith. For the joy set before him he endured the cross, scorning its shame, and sat down at the right hand of the throne of God. Consider him who endured such opposition from sinners, so that you will not grow weary and lose heart.
> **Hebrews 12:1-3**

The Kingdom of God has been resisted for 2,000 years but it has advanced. Now that the king is coming, the resistance is escalating to alarming levels. I suggest we stand UNDIVIDED.

Todd Starnes sums it up in his recent book *God Less America*, "The storm clouds are gathering. The winds of revolution are blowing, friends. Religious liberty is under attack." [2]

Tony Perkins, president of the Family Research Council and Liberty's Institute's Jeff Mateer, noted that while in 2012, their religious liberty study documented 600 examples of hostility towards people of faith, that number rocketed to nearly 1,200 documented cases of religious liberty violations in 2013.[3]

In the book *God Less America*, Frank Page, president of the Southern Baptist Convention Executive Committee, warned of a bleak future for Christians in America. "I'm not a conspiracy theorist but I do believe the day is coming when churches will see outright persecution, as well as, a continued pattern of harassment and marginalization in this culture. Churches better gear up and realize that day is coming."[4]

> Silence the Church, remove moral restraints and it's a near turn-key operation for world dominance.

Dr. Page goes on to say, "There will be active and open persecution because of the biblical worldview of churches... When you have national leaders who say Baptists and other evangelicals are guilty of hate speech because of our recitation of simple scripture, then you are going to see the alienation and active persecution of churches in the United States."[5]

In 2013, the IRS audited The Billy Graham Evangelistic Association. Why? Franklin Graham believes it is because of their sponsorship role in promoting traditional marriage. In 2009, in Fort Bend County, Texas, the IRS forced pro-life groups to reveal the content of their prayers before receiving tax exempt status. This is both mind-boggling and intimidating. Allan Blume, editor of the Biblical Recorder, the official news journal for the North Carolina Baptist State Convention, believes something is not right. "There seems to be a very anti-Christian bias that has flowed into a lot of government agencies — oppression literally against Christian organizations and groups. It makes you wonder what's going on."[6]

The website www.speakupmovement.org, sponsored by Alliance Defense Freedom, offers encouragement and assistance to Christians facing this new antagonism towards biblical truth. "There are numerous accounts of Christians who are facing legal trials and tribulations simply for abiding by their religious convictions. Perhaps these accounts demonstrate why Christians today have a real foreboding sense that persecution is coming. They've heard the stories and see the possibility in a culture that is increasingly hostile to Christianity. And they see the cultural disapproval and hostility increasing at a startlingly rapid pace."[7]

The great and respected apologist, Ravi Zacharias notices the growing anti-Christian mood of our progressively secular world. "Sadly, over the years, the Christian faith has been targeted by a rabid secularization and evicted from any or all public expression. The encroachment upon our civil liberties is frightening and we ought to take a stand." [8]

Dr. Michael Youssef, president of Leading the Way Ministries also expresses his belief that Christian persecution is becoming more mainstream to silence the Church. "If Christians in a social gathering, or on the Piers Morgan show, say they believe Jesus is the only Savior and Lord, they will incite the most venomous verbal attack. If Christians speak out against Islamism or the celebration of homosexuality, they will be attacked with labels such as "Islamophobe" or "homophobe"— words manufactured by two groups that would normally hate each other but join forces for the purpose of eliminating the true Christian point of view." [9]

The tribulation experienced by Christians around the globe far exceeds the level of legal challenges or verbal harassment the American Church is starting to face. However, this spirit of Anti-Christ is on a global hunt. The American Church, once the dominant international Christian voice, is scared to speak. Without coincidence, the anti-christian spirit becomes emboldened in its cruel measures to imprison Christians, decapitate converts and burn sanctuaries. High profile cases, such as Pastor Saeed, unjustly imprisoned in Iran and Meriam Yehya Ibrahim, the young Sudanese mother sentenced to death for apostasy because she refused to recant her Christian faith, will cause a temporary international outcry. The Church is left praying and petitioning, while Presidents and Prime Ministers dismiss their role in resolving these Human Rights violations. According to a 2014 Pew Research Study, Christians lead the way as the most persecuted religious group in the world. [10]

Historically and currently, oppressive nations from those under Islamic Sharia Law to Communism, have trampled religious freedom. Primarily, because religious liberty was an American ideal which gave rise to the movement of justice and liberty. For centuries, including Western Civilization, your 'Christian' faith was that of the monarchy that ruled your land. The Pilgrims charted a new course. A path of independence where the individual's conscience dictated faith and worship, not the Church of England or the King of England.

In defense of Hobby Lobby's decision to oppose the Affordable Care Act's mandatory requirement for businesses to provide controversial, contraception abortion pills, Pastor Rick Warren appealed to the Religious Liberty of these sanctified Separatists who landed on Plymouth Rock. "The first people who came to America from Europe were devout pilgrims seeking the freedom to practice their faith. That's why the first phrase of the first sentence of the First Amendment is about freedom of religion — preceding freedom of speech, freedom of the press and freedom of assembly. Why? Because if you don't have the freedom to live and practice what you believe, the other freedoms are irrelevant. Religious liberty is America's First Freedom."[11]

In unparalleled brilliance, Satan has redefined freedom of religion and subverted it with freedom to worship. This is to say, our ability to sing three songs, collect money, announce the men's breakfast and listen to encouraging practical teaching, is not threatened by the anti-Christian spirit. However, persecution is immediate and combative when the Christian engages his sphere of influence with a biblical worldview.

Author and cultural commentator, Eric Metaxas said, "They have freedom of worship in China and they had it in Germany in the 1930s. Today, that is what we have—freedom of worship. So today, we are slowly privatizing our faith because of this great misunderstanding. Once we leave our homes or our churches, we are expected to accept the secular humanist view of everything." [12]

I briefly covered the views and opinions of leading Christian voices to substantiate my argument that a militaristic, anti-Christian spirit is noticeably agitated and antagonizing the Church. The influence of this spirit goes beyond the IRS targeting Christian groups or the Affordable Health Care Act forcing believers to violate their conscience. It is now leveraging its power in our military. The loss of money through the pressure of the IRS or the loss of one's business due to not following immoral secular laws would persuade numerous American Christians to disavow Christ. What happens when the power of the sword, the administrators of justice, unjustly mistreat and mislabel the Church?

The Family Research Council's publication, *Clear and Present Danger*, published December 13, 2013, highlights over 50 cases in less than three years of religious hostility towards Christians serving in the military or the views of the military brass regarding the Christian church in America. The most prominent 'thorn in the flesh' is the Military Religious Freedom Foundation, led by anti-christian activist Mikey Weinstein. A fraction of recent violations include:

Chaplain is ordered to remove a religion-themed essay from USAF base website – July 24, 2013

Lt. Col. Kenneth Reyes, a chaplain at Joint Base Elmendorf-Richardson (JBER) in Alaska, was told to remove a religious essay that he posted on the base website. The essay was entitled, "No Atheists in Foxholes: Chaplains Gave all in World War II" referring to a comment made by Father William Cummings, a Catholic priest, who observed "[t]here is no such thing as an atheist in a foxhole." President Eisenhower repeated the phrase during a speech to the American Legion in 1954. Mikey Weinstein's MRFF sent a demand letter to JBER's commander, Col. Brian P. Duffy, claiming to represent 42 anonymous service members assigned there who were offended by the post. MRFF claimed, "through redundant use of the bigoted, religious supremacist phrase, 'no atheists in foxholes,' he defiles the dignity of service members." The essay was taken down within five hours of receipt of the complaint. MRFF wanted the chaplain to be reprimanded. However, Col. Reyes' article was restored to the base website in mid-August with a disclaimer placed on the site.

An Army assistant chaplain is threatened for sharing her biblical beliefs on homosexuality via Facebook – August 6, 2013

An Army chaplain's assistant, stationed near Colorado Springs, Colorado was ordered to remove a Facebook post or face disciplinary action including, possibly, a reduction in rank and pay. One Sunday evening, the airman was listening to a pastor endorse homosexuality. Afterward, she posted on her Facebook page her frustrations with pastors endorsing homosexuality and denying it to be a sin. Her commander called her into his office on Monday and asked that she remove the post because it created a "hostile and antagonistic" environment. Intense pressure was placed upon her after her pastor, Todd Hudnall (Radiant Church), made the Army's actions known to the public. She removed this posting to her personal Facebook page.

Department of Defense training materials suggest conservative viewpoints are "extremist" – August 22, 2013

A Judicial Watch Freedom of Information Act request produced Department of Defense (DOD) anti-discrimination training materials implying that some conservative organizations are "hate groups." Students were told to be aware that "many extremists will talk of individual liberties, states' rights, and how to make the world a better place." The documents repeatedly cited the leftwing Southern Poverty Law Center (SPLC) as a resource for identifying "hate groups." One document suggested that the American colonists who rebelled against British rule were members of an "extremist movement."

Air Force Senior Master Sergeant Phillip Monk is relieved of duties over gay marriage – July 25, 2013; files complaint – August 20, 2013; is given a Miranda warning by Air Force investigator – August 27, 2013

A 19-year veteran of the Air Force, Senior Master Sergeant Phillip Monk, was relieved of his duties after he disagreed with his openly gay commander, Maj. Elisa Valenzuela, when she wanted to severely punish an instructor who had expressed religious objections to homosexuality. Valenzuela incorrectly told Monk that opposition to same-sex marriage constituted discrimination. Monk disagreed. Valenzuela relieved Monk of his duties as First Sergeant for the unit. Monk was also placed on restricted liberty and was no longer permitted to be physically present in the unit's buildings or facilities located at Lackland Air Force Base, San Antonio, TX. News of these events broke around mid-August 2013, and Monk filed a formal complaint against Valenzuela on August 20, 2013. In an August 27, 2013, meeting with an Air Force investigator, Sgt. Monk and his attorney, Michael Berry (Liberty Institute), were told that Monk is under investigation criminally for violating Article 107 of the Uniform Code of Military Justice (UCMJ)—making a false official statement. Monk was read his Miranda rights at that time. This step was puzzling because Monk had made no official comments on this matter—an essential element of an Article 107 violation. The Air Force action appeared to be retaliation for Monk's discrimination filing against Major Valenzuela.

Fort Hood, TX briefing describes evangelical Christians as a threat-October 17, 2013

On October 17, 2013, soldiers attended a counter-intelligence pre-deployment briefing at Fort Hood, Texas during which they were told that evangelical Christians and members of the Tea Party threatened the country. Additionally, they were informed that soldiers who donated to such organizations could be subject to discipline under the Uniform Code of Military Justice. According to sources, the counter-intelligence officer leading the briefing spent approximately thirty minutes discussing the ways evangelical Christians, generally, and groups like the American Family Association, specifically, were "tearing the country apart."

Top officials at the Pentagon insist these 50+ incidents are isolated and do not reflect Military policy. I agree with the policy defense, but indirectly, the spirit of Anti-Christ homogenizes such actions to work in one accord. Could America's military be in the early stages of transformation to indoctrinate privates with false views of Conservative Christian groups, while simultaneously creating an environment where Christian evangelization is not permitted and a biblical world view is excluded?

Throughout history, when a government fails, they locate the weakest and most intolerable group to cast the blame. Hitler condemned the Jews. Nero incriminated the Christians. As America continues to decline, could the Christian faithful be the next fringed group, ostracized from the mainstream and from the military?

Roman Emperor Diocletian ordered the most horrifying and torturous persecution in the history of the Church. After losing battles in Persia, his generals informed him that the army was defeated because Rome neglected the gods. A return to Roman gods and goddess worship was mandatory for all military personal, including Christians! Of course, they did not comply with the emperor's edict. Christians had to recant their faith or withdraw from the Roman forces. Within a few years, Diocletian purged all Christians out of the military. He then, promptly, used his new non-Christian military to force all of Rome to worship the old gods and goddesses. He revoked the tolerance decree issues by Emperor Gallienus on 260AD. [13] Could the US military turn against the Church within her homeland?

Focus on the Family's Dr. James Dobson circulated an editorial letter from Congressman Tim Huelskamp, the First District of Kansas, in his August 2013 newsletter Freedom, Justice and Religious Liberty for All. He focuses specifically on what the Commander-in-Chief and his senior officers are doing to the U.S. military. The following is part of that letter:

> With the exceptions of free enterprise and traditional marriage, no institution has been more "radically transformed" by the Obama regime than our Armed Forces. Given President Obama's notorious contempt for Americans who "cling to their Bibles" and "guns," perhaps we shouldn't be surprised by his Administration's hostility to service members who espouse traditional Judeo-Christian beliefs.

> The persecution of Christians and conservatives has become increasingly brazen and pervasive since the President took office four and one half years ago. To "protect patients" from proselytizing or prayer, Walter Reed Army Medical Center banned wounded warriors' family members from "bringing or using Bibles" during visits. The Department of Veterans Affairs barred Christian prayers at a National Cemetery. The President signed the law that repealed "Don't Ask, Don't Tell." The Attorney General refused to defend the Defense of Marriage Act (DOMA) in court and the Department of Defense authorized unholy "matrimony" ceremonies at military installations even before the Supreme Court struck down part of DOMA. [14]

Meanwhile, Former Arkansas Governor Mike Huckabee also commented in August of 2013, in his newsletter Stop Discriminating Against Christians, "Christian soldiers, sailors and airmen are told to put away their Bibles, and remove any Christian references from their personal Facebook pages. Chaplains are ordered not to pray in the name of Jesus, and even to take down signs that quote President Eisenhower's saying, '"There are no atheists in foxholes,"' because that might be offensive to atheists. It would appear that if some in the military had their way, there would be no Christians or Jews in foxholes, because they'd be systematically drummed out of the military. Look, I think we should accommodate people who adhere to Islam, Hinduism or Judaism and who serve in the military. The First Amendment is all about the freedom to believe, worship, express, even disagree. But why are Christians in the armed services singled out for discrimination?"

I sense the anti-Christ spirit breathing down the necks of Christians. The government is clearly slanted in opposition to the Church. As alluded to earlier, the IRS targets our organizations in an unconstitutional manner, in conjunction with Congress and the Administration passing unconstitutional laws. The spirit of lawlessness disregards the law, specifically the US Constitution in the areas of religious liberty and religious free speech.

There is one trademark sin that encapsulates all the forcefulness and belligerence of the anti-Christian lawless spirit — sexual immorality and specifically homosexuality. I think the evidence is convincing. Primarily, sexual laws are being changed and biblical speech, regarding sexuality, is being banned.

Todd Starnes comments, "I believe we are just a few years away from American pastors being brought up on charges of hate speech against homosexuals. I believe we will see attempts made to shut down churches and remove Bibles from public libraries — all because of what the scriptures teach about homosexuality." [15]

If ever there was a blasphemous and sacrilegious three-fold cord, this is it: Spirit of Lawlessness, Spirit of Anti-Christ, Spirit of Homosexuality. Please understand my intentions and definitions. I am not grouping the male or female who struggles with same sex attraction with the Gay Rights Agenda which is prevailing in our nation and at the cost of religious liberty. It would be hard for the most liberal of defenses to ignore the connection between the marriage laws that are being changed and the anti-Christian opinion towards biblical teaching, with respect to same sex committed relationships and homosexual lifestyles.

The fear of retribution towards the traditional Christian belief of marriage has led many ministers to back-peddle and avoid any statement on the issue with clarity. 'Jesus never spoke about it... I suggest neither should we.' Equally, Jesus never spoke about being saved by grace. Paul did, and he addressed homosexual practices as an apostle to the Gentiles. In order not to contradict the 'Jesus words only' philosophical approach to ministry, there should be less focus on hyper-grace and more on self-denial. Finally, Jesus' audience had a thorough understanding of sexuality taught graphically in the Law of Moses. The Gentiles required a renewal of the mind in this area, similar to half of America.

First, most Americans now approve of same sex marriage. This is a dramatic change within the past decade. The most recent Gallup Poll dated May 21, 2014, states that 55% of Americans now support this alternative definition of family. [16] That is an all time high. Not surprisingly, 80% of young adults support same sex marriage. Did I mention that only 1% of this group has a biblical worldview? Somewhat, but not completely surprising, is the research from Baylor University that found 24% of Evangelical Christians were "ambivalent," meaning they support the legal recognition of same sex marriage, though personally, morally opposing it. [17]

Same sex marriage is the current step, on an otherwise long progressive path to a post-Christian, secular, global world. For the past decade, this debate centered on the practicality of a biblical worldview as the boundary of marriage. The current discussion is how to balance religious liberty when the teaching of that religion is fundamentally at odds with the secular blessing of sexual immorality. If forecasters are accurate, religious liberty will lose this upcoming case, both in the legal courts and of public opinion.

Chai Feldblum, President Obama's commissioner for the Equal Employment Opportunity Commission, believes 'identity liberty' (sexual orientation) takes preeminence over 'belief liberty' (religious freedom). "...in making the decision in this zero sum game, I am convinced society should come down on the side of protecting the liberty of LGBT people...Protecting one group's identity liberty may, at times, require that we burden others' belief liberty. This is an inherent and irreconcilable reality of our complex society." [18]

Todd Starnes reported in 2013, on the case of a New Mexico photographer who was found in violation by the New Mexico Supreme Court of the state's Human Rights Act, for not photographing a same sex wedding. The judge ruled that businesses are compelled by law to compromise the very religious beliefs that inspire their lives. Owner and photographer, Aaron Klein comments, "It's a sad day for Christian business owners and it's a sad day for the First Amendment." [19]

Ken Klukowski, the director for the Center for Religious Liberty at the Family Research Council stated, "This decision would stun the framers of the U.S. Constitution, it's a gross violation of the First Amendment and should now be taken up by the U.S. Supreme Court to reaffirm the basic principle that the fundamental rights of free speech and the free exercise of religion do not stop at the exit door of your local church and instead extend to every area of a religious person's life,... this is forcing religious Americans to violate the basic teachings of their faith, or lose their jobs." [20]

Fifty-two percent of Americans believe that businesses providing wedding services should be forced to participate in same sex weddings, even if the owner has religious objections. [21] Charles Haynes, director of the Religious Freedom Education Project said, "According to the latest numbers, most citizens now believe that our commitment to non-discrimination must trump religious objections to homosexuality in the public square of America." [22]

Family Research Council's President, Tony Perkins emphasizes the end of religious liberty verses sexual liberty, "What's becoming ever so clear to those who thought homosexual activists could be appeased is that their ultimate goal is to sanitize the public space of anyone who holds to a biblical worldview of morality." [23]

This is why NY Times Columnist, Ross Douthat wants to make amends and agree to the 'terms of surrender' before its too late. "... pressure would be brought to bear wherever the religious subculture brushed up against state power. Religious-affiliated adoption agencies would be closed if they declined to place children with same-sex couples. (This has happened in Massachusetts and Illinois.) Organizations and businesses that promoted the older definition of marriage would face constant procedural harassment, along the lines suggested by the mayors who battled with Chick-fil-A. And, eventually, religious schools and colleges would receive the same treatment as racist holdouts like Bob Jones University, losing access to public funds and seeing their tax-exempt status revoked." [24]

I could belabor the point and mention Pastor Louie Giglio, who was invited to lead the prayer at President Obama's Inauguration but was forced to withdraw because of a twenty year old sermon that taught a biblical worldview concerning sexuality. I could bring up African American Pastor Donnie McClurkin, who was invited to perform at the

50th anniversary of the civil rights movement in Washington D.C. but was 'disinvited' after gay activists protested his involvement, since he testifies about being delivered from the curse of homosexuality. Phil Robertson, of Duck Dynasty fame, had a public image debacle because of his views concerning normal sexuality. Brendan Eich, CEO of Firefox was forced to resign because he supported traditional marriage in 2008, even though President Obama held similar beliefs that year.

These incidents are a snapshot of a monumental problem on the horizon for the Church. The days are darkening. Public opinion is against us. Times have changed but the Bible has not. The celebrations of Palm Sunday are past and not returning. This is our Good Friday. The Church is facing a trial and judgement at the hands of men. As the Pharisees changed the attitudes of the people against Christ by controlling the flow and freedom of information during his arrest, so the elites who control the belief systems of our culture through government, media and the schools have equally done the same in our world.

The Spirit of Lawlessness changed laws concerning sexuality. The Spirit of Anti-Christ changed the public's position against the Church. The Spirit of Homosexuality changed freedom of religion to freedom of worship and insists on silence and submission. These three dominant and combative spirits are preparing the world for the man of lawlessness, the Anti-Christ, the sexually immoral global leader, who will usher in a progressive global government — the one envisioned by the humanists, atheists and statists for decades. All this made possible, because America turned away from the faith — the 5 Core Beliefs of a Christian worldview and removed all moral restraints in the process.

These are the days of Noah and the days of Lot.

As it was in the days of Noah, so it will be at the
coming of the Son of Man.
Matthew 24:37

Just as it was in the days of Noah, so also will it be in the days
of the Son of Man. People were eating, drinking, marrying and
being given in marriage up to the day Noah entered the ark.
Then the flood came and destroyed them all. It was the same
in the days of Lot. People were eating and drinking, buying and

selling, planting and building. But the day Lot left Sodom, fire and sulfur rained down from heaven and destroyed them all.
Luke 17:26-29

If he did not spare the ancient world when he brought the flood on its ungodly people, but protected Noah, a preacher of righteousness, and seven others; if he condemned the cities of Sodom and Gomorrah by burning them to ashes, and made them an example of what is going to happen to the ungodly; and if he rescued Lot, a righteous man, who was distressed by the depraved conduct of the lawless (for that righteous man, living among them day after day, was tormented in his righteous soul by the lawless deeds he saw and heard)
2 Peter 2:5-8

...they deliberately forget that long ago by God's word the heavens came into being and the earth was formed out of water and by water. By these waters also the world of that time was deluged and destroyed. By the same word the present heavens and earth are reserved for fire, being kept for the day of judgment and destruction of the ungodly.
2 Peter 3:5-7

Jesus and Peter communicated the similarities of the spirit which was in the world during the time of Noah and Lot, to the spirit that would be prevalent and recklessly running rampant in the last days — the spirit of sexual immorality. Noah and Lot lived in overindulgent, sexual cultures which had no respect for godly marriages or gender identities. The context of Genesis 6, the biblical account of Noah, places him in a society which redefined marriage.

When human beings began to increase in number on the earth and daughters were born to them, the sons of God saw that the daughters of humans were beautiful, and they married any of them they chose. Then the Lord said, "My Spirit will not contend with humans forever, for they are mortal; their days will be a hundred and twenty years." The Nephilim were on the earth in those days—and also afterward—when the sons of God went to the daughters of humans and had children by them.

They were the heroes of old, men of renown.
Genesis 6:1-4

'Married any of them they chose,' was the cause of the effect —
judgement, as God said, "My Spirit will not contend with humans forever..." Lot, faired even worse, as he was tormented by lawless deeds
and threatened by the spirit of sexual immorality.

> ...all the men from every part of the city of Sodom—both young
> and old—surrounded the house. They called to Lot, "Where are
> the men who came to you tonight? Bring them out to us so that
> we can have sex with them."
> **Genesis 19:4-5**

This spirit has surfaced again with the power to be more convincing and with unparalleled aggression. For the most part, deception has
been fairly smooth. Question the Christian faith and test the strength of
the Church. As biblical belief declined, sexual restraints were loosened.
The sexual spirit is now free to roam, while the gospel is fearfully bound
behind pulpits.

The strategy has worked — and woe to the inhabitants of the
earth. The man of lawlessness will be accepted and celebrated without
any hinderance or criticism. For he is the face of the lawless, anti-
Christian, homosexual spirit. In Revelation, the city of Jerusalem is
called Sodom in the spirit, after this man hijacks the temple as his
place of worship.

> ...the great city—which is figuratively called Sodom and
> Egypt—where also their Lord was crucified.
> **Revelation 11:8**

Sodom is the most significant biblical, geographical term for homosexuality, as Egypt is the place of idolatry and the bondage or persecution
of God's people. Clearly, Jerusalem will be the centerpiece of the anti-
Christian homosexual stronghold.

> (He)...had a mouth which spoke pompous words,
> whose appearance was greater than his fellows.
> **Daniel 7:20 NKJV**

This description of the beast in Daniel bears witness to the beast of Revelation. Just as the Egyptian pharaohs believed in their own divinity, so the beast speaks boastful words of idolatry. In this verse, he is described as being more handsome and seductive than his intimate fellows and friends, more aptly characterized as 'feminine men.' Daniel 7:20 is the sole time in Scripture when the translated word for 'associates, fellows, companions' is the Aramaic word *chabrah* — the feminine noun, in contrast to the masculine *chabar*. Daniel was inspired by the Holy Spirit to make the appropriate differentiation.

Furthermore, Daniel writes:

- This beast will change the laws (Daniel 7:25 — spirit of lawlessness)

- This beast will oppose the people of God (Daniel 7:21 — spirit of anti-Christ)

- This beast will have no desire for women (Daniel 11:37 — spirit of homosexuality)

Furthermore, the Apostle John writes that this beast will trample on long held, religious liberty and pressure all to worship him or be excluded from business, economic transactions, and job opportunities. (Revelation 13:16-17, the court of public opinion currently supports such beliefs. There will be a deafening silence in protest for religious rights.) The anti-covenant agenda is advancing. Anti-Christian, anti-Israeli, and anti-marriage movements are well received on university campuses and social media.

I presume this chapter has been the most challenging, most uncomfortable and most uncertain to digest. As opposing worldviews continue to weaken the moral strength of a nation by progressively eliminating the Christian faith to prepare the masses to embrace the world community, the spirits exposed in this chapter are seducing and desensitizing the masses to embrace the leader of that global community. The end of the Church Age is rapidly approaching. The timeline exhibited by the crucified body of Jesus prompts us to stand and proclaim Christ and our core beliefs — UNDIVIDED.

Author's Note:

To be clear, my personal convictions concerning this eschatological spiritual shift does not reflect the views of other pastors and churches. Secondly, every individual, regardless of sexual orientation, must be afforded compassion, love, kindness, respect and dignity. God explicitly and unequivocally offers redemption and forgiveness to all. I know the depth of my sin which requires His grace. Uncovering the spirit of this age and the bearing it will have upon the Church should inspire action, not infer judgment.

Chapter Eleven

The Urgency of the Hour

Now, brothers and sisters, about times and dates
we do not need to write to you, for you know very well that the
day of the Lord will come like a thief in the night.
While people are saying, "Peace and safety,"
destruction will come on them suddenly, as labor pains on a
pregnant woman, and they will not escape.
But you, brothers and sisters, are not in darkness so that this
day should surprise you like a thief.
You are all children of the light and children of the day.
1 Thessalonians 5:1-5

"But take heed to yourselves, lest your hearts be weighed down
with carousing, drunkenness, and cares of this life,
and that Day come on you unexpectedly.
For it will come as a snare on all those who dwell on the face of
the whole earth. Watch therefore, and pray always that you may
be counted worthy to escape all these things that will come to
pass, and to stand before the Son of Man."
Luke 21:34-36

…the end of all things is at hand;
therefore be serious and watchful in your prayers.
1 Peter 4:7

…the day of the Lord will come as a thief in the night…
2 Peter 3:10

Therefore you also be ready, for the Son of Man is coming
at an hour you do not expect.
Luke 12:40

Behold, I am coming as a thief. Blessed is he who watches…
Revelation 16:15

"What are we doing for spring break this year? I don't want to sit home. Can we go somewhere?" Endless words of future boredom and puppy-eyed whining would nag at me for two weeks before my children started their Easter break on Good Friday. My offspring organized and unanimously petitioned the head of the house to go anywhere during their seven day rest from academic responsibility, minus the book reports that are scheduled to be completed a few days after any major school break. I thought of different places, some near and some far, but time and money hindered dreams and destinations.

As spring break drew near, I started to feel a slight tug in my heart to take the children on a day trip to Washington, D.C. Long drives and overpopulated tourism was never my thing. I have been to D.C. many times before but only once with my children and most of them, too young to recall such precious memories. Grace must be afforded to them.

I remember that first trip, years ago, very well. The walk from the Capitol building to the White House seemed inhumane as my two and three-year-olds kept pulling down on my hand to stop our forward momentum. Granted, they were young. "C'mon, they're older now," I said to myself. I was not convinced and just the thought of the trip made me more anxious than excited. The "what are we doing, where are we going" question made me feel trapped. Since I'm well versed in the political sciences, I gave the typical cabinet member before a Congressional Committee answer — "I don't know."

Behind the scenes, I mentioned to my wife, Glennys, about the slight possibility of a family outing to the nation's capitol. Spring break started, Easter weekend ended and the end of the vacation week was two moons away. My wife texted me because she needed a final answer for her job, as she would not be able to work Saturday. I was reluctant to commit either way. Honestly, I was trying to find a reason not to go.

Then all of a sudden, I had this strong nudge inside of me. The still small voice of our God saying, "There is something you need to see, there is something you need to hear." Reluctancy turned to relief. I had a final answer. "Yes, my love. We are going." I informed the children and briefed them on the walking duties and distances. This trip was going to be different!

The early Saturday morning of April 26, 2014, arrived. Coffee before sunrise, a small breakfast as a road trip was on the agenda and a quick prayer to reflect and seek the face of God. "Lord, I don't know why I am doing this. I really don't want to go but I know that You are sending me there. There is something You want me to see and something You want me to hear. Please guide me so I don't miss it. Please make sure I see it and hear it." My wife never knew about this impromptu direction from the Lord or my private bedchamber prayer to Him. What if I was wrong and there was nothing to see or hear? As a minister, I am conservative about the voice of God. I dare not look foolish by claiming 'God said,' when in reality it was 'Shawn thought.' For spiritual safety reasons, I meditated on this guiding instruction deep in my heart.

The drive was going exceptionally well. Just over an hour before arrival, my wife looked at me from the passenger seat and said these surprising but reassuring words, "I don't know why we are going here. Maybe it is just a fun family day to be with the kids. If that is all it is, great. That's fine but I feel as though we are going for another reason. God told me that He is in this. I don't know what that means but in prayer He told me, 'I am in this.' I think there is something He wants to show us." My eyes instantly opened to cartoon-like character measurements, as what I heard from the Lord two days prior and repeated in prayer earlier that morning was confirmed in her now. "I feel the same thing! I believe God is leading us here because 'there is something I need to see and something I need to hear.'" Expectations now exploded in our spirits. We drove with a renewed sense of energy and focus.

The original plan was to use the Metro system near the outer belt but an audible was called by the navigator, my wife, to park ourselves at Union Station — the transportation hub of the most powerful political city in the world. We arrived earlier than planned and quickly made our way to the Capitol for some landscape family photographs. That which I feared the most came upon me — one child transformed this man of faith into his father in the flesh by these migraine-inspiring words, "I can't walk anymore. Can we go home? I am tired." Three blocks! This is not an exaggeration — three blocks, and my son was throwing in the towel and interrupting my spiritual pilgrimage. Needless to say, I wasn't very sympathetic or accommodating to his request. We were not going home. I coached him and all my children for days on the amount of walking that would be expected.

The disappointment steamrolled downhill. My son's constant refusal to walk and verbal cries to rest quenched any faith and fire I had. The crowd of thousands upon our arrival quickly multiplied to tens of thousands, which hindered the ability to view most museums and monuments. The temperature of the day was quickly rising and an incredibly long line of people wrapped around the corner of Constitution Avenue. The crowd which encircled the National Archive building was enough to make an angel feel human. I was done. My wife, seeing my frustration and overwhelmed by the heat, said those supportive words I was desperate for, "Let's go home."

Grudgingly, I trudged my family back to Union Station. I argued with God in my head the entire walk back. Thank God for His grace. He handled my complaining much better than I handled my son's complaining. "What a wasted trip! I was so wrong for thinking You sent me here. There was nothing to see! There was nothing to hear! I wasted my time. I wasted my money. The kids don't want to walk. It's horrible. What a horrible trip! Never again!" The devotional prayer at sunrise morphed into the ill-tempered prayer by mid afternoon. Block by block, we would rest and go for thirty minutes until returning back to Union Station.

Crossing Columbus Circle, we entered the home stretch through the doors and into the lobby. Immediately, after three steps into the building, one more unforeseen roadblock would extend our trip. Sirens, strobe lights and an annoying emergency squeal flooded Union Station. "An emergency has been reported. Evacuate the building immediately. This is an emergency. Evacuate the building," ordered the overhead speakers! Quickly, I looked around and to my surprise, everyone seemed clueless to the ear-splitting instructions. People continued to sit and eat their chicken wraps and sip their iced teas. I looked at my wife and said, "What do we do?" She replied, "Get out. This could be dangerous." As we abruptly reversed course, another family entered

Union Station. They paused as the visual and audible signals were blaring full force. I, being Captain Obvious, informed them, "There is an emergency. Everyone has to leave." They stared at me for one second, ignoring the alarms and my Good Samaritan interaction and continued through the atrium and into the shops.

Outside, feeling somewhat foolish and possibly overreactive, we patiently waited. The post-9/11 transportation hub of Washington, D.C. was having an emergency but no one evacuated, no one cared. Instead of people leaving, even more were ignorantly and stubbornly walking inside, passing the alarms and sirens echoing near the street corner, while fire trucks came blaring down Constitution Avenue. After four minutes, the attitude changed and countless crowds filed out of the building orderly and casually. I looked at my oldest son (shaking my head) and said, "This is what's wrong with America. Everyone thinks they're too cool. Nothing is ever going to happen to them. It's always someone else on the news story but never them. Just go slow, take it easy, be cool, you're the man. If the alarm is going off and instructions are clear, why not just leave?" I was taking advantage of this as a teachable moment. I continued to complain about humanity and the situation at hand, "Where are the cops? Where is security? No one is telling people to get out. No one is stopping anyone from going in. And that's another problem! People won't move unless someone in authority tells them. C'mon folks, just listen to the alarms and instructions."

Having a cool story to tell others about our emergency experience in D.C. made the inconvenience of a twenty minute wait time more enjoyable. Eventually, the alarms ceased and crowds reentered, though not by authoritative personnel. They were still strangely absent from my vantage point. Hesitantly, we followed the broad road and headed towards our vehicle.

With the air conditioner on max and our GPS set, we embarked on the return trip. Before the first traffic light, the children were passed out asleep. A little bit of quiet did me good. Excuse the vulnerability but I was 'in the flesh,' upset, agitated and resentful for my burning bush "go to D.C." whirlwind fantasy that collided into reality. My pleasant wife, who soothes my soul during stressful moments, did her job perfectly as she slowly faded into an exhausted nap. Many miles and myself was all I had.

I was trekking out of the D.C. area and into Maryland when God enlightened my understanding. The atmosphere in the car shifted as peace and holiness swelled up tears in my eyes. I felt the presence of my Savior. It was tangible and it is rare. "You have seen what you needed to see. You have heard what you needed to hear. That is why I sent you, remember?" In awe and openness I responded with the simple "Yes, Lord." Then our God placed His burden in my heart and stirred my soul with uncompromising zeal. "Remember Union Station. There was no sense of urgency. There was an overwhelming and dangerous false sense of security. This nation and my Church within this nation, has no sense of urgency but a false sense of security. That is why the Bible says, when people are saying 'peace and safety' sudden destruction will come upon them. The people ignored the sirens and alarms. This nation and even my people within this nation are ignoring the signs of the times, just as those people in Union Station, knowing their uncertain safety of being in Washington DC, ignored the alarms, the strobe lights and the overhead instructions." God continued to say, "Tell my people that we cannot depend on the signs of the times to awaken and shake the world, knowing my return is coming. They will ignore the signs. Did you see anyone in authority telling people to leave or stopping them from going in?" "No, Lord," I replied. "Those in authority were too busy trying to stop the alarm. They thought people would respond to the sound, the lights, the overhead instructions but when there is a false spirit of peace and safety, people will ignore the signs. People need someone in authority to come and tell them to 'get out.' Tell my people the time of urgency and the time to speak with authority is now. For this nation is living under a false sense of security and I am coming soon."

God sent me four hundred miles, used my son to dictate the pace of our trip and took advantage of my frustrated weakness, to stop me from strolling around D.C. with my spiritual antennas searching for heaven's signal. However, the steps of a good man are ordered by the Lord (Psalm 37:23). I had seen what I needed to see and heard what I needed to hear.

I concede, I was spiritually frustrated for months before our trip. I launched "We Stand UNDIVIDED" on January 25, 2014, at the NJ Statehouse with three words rolling around in my belly — passion, urgency, and authority. I prayed over sermon materials to formulate a key message for this new campaign. For the life of me, I could not communicate the appeal for urgency and authority. As a tagline, it worked. Practically, the words were empty and powerless. I fasted and prayed for forty days leading up to a special Move the Earth partner night on April 10, as I would confidently share the message "We Stand UNDIVIDED." I was earnestly seeking the Lord and searching the scriptures for the meat of this prophetic call to action. April 10th passed by and though I had words on paper, nothing clicked and no peace rested in my spirit. That is, until April 26th, when God spoke,

> 'There is no sense of urgency, but a dangerous and false sense of security....people will ignore the signs until someone in authority tells them to get out."

My dear brothers and sisters, the days are short. The time is now. This is no ordinary day as we are not living in ordinary times. Gruelingly, I wrote ten chapters in hopes of educating, informing and causing an awareness within the Church of the worldviews and spirits that are actively resisting the Kingdom of God and our soon coming King. Now I plead with you, I implore you in the name of Christ to preach with authority for this is the hour of urgency! Our awakening has come! We must swiftly make His path ready with the authority we have been delegated.

"Let us thunder forth the law and Gospel of God until our voices reach the capital of this nation, through our representatives in Congress. Let us give the reporters of the press such work to do as will make their ears and the ears of their readers tingle...We need more sons of thunder in the pulpit. We need men that will flash forth the law of God like livid lightning and arouse the consciences of men," Charles Finney.

'There is no sense of urgency, but a dangerous and false sense of security...

Could it be that our reliance upon technology and psychology, rooted in secular eduction, has given us academic avenues to improve the worship experience and message points but in the process, we misplaced our exclusive uniqueness of absolute truth? Has the thought police bullied the Church into a corner of spiritual crisis and confusion?

"Our goal should be to be innocent of the blood of all men by preaching the full counsel of God... Some say, 'we don't get involved in controversial things, we only preach the gospel.' That is an oxymoron, because the gospel is controversial...If we are all willing to go to jail, then none of us will have to," Dr. Richard Lamb at the 2013 Watchmen of the Wall Conference.

The sound of angels and the hoof prints of heaven are becoming louder. The King of Glory is readying His armies. No man knows the day or the hour. I insist that we live as if revival and the coming of Christ will happen in our lifetime, for the Bible insists that Christians in all time periods remain alert and ready for the Lord's return (Matthew 24:36, Romans 13:11, 1 Corinthians 7:29, 10:11, 15:51,52, Philippians 4:5).

This is not a post-modern evangelical call to *separatism*. God forbid we forsake His command to 'occupy and do business' until he comes (Luke 19:13). I am your typical biblical worldview teacher — redeem the culture and influence the seven spheres of society with your Christian faith. Above all, the Church as mentioned in chapter 10, is called to hold back and restrain these spirits from deceiving, deluding and decaying this world. The Kingdom of God has come. God forgive us if we forfeit it.

I am an unyielding advocate of Christian *activism*. The government is on the top level of cultural influence. Did not God set up and commission the powers of human government? Should God's voice not be heard in the halls of Congress that, through Providence, He made possible? Nonetheless, that's not the unction of my shout!

"We Stand UNDIVIDED" is a call to urgency and unity! The Church must return to her first love with purity and passion; a passion for the written word and a passion for the living word. The Church has become dumb and dry. Our people need an education in the Word and an encounter with the Word. The Apostle Paul offers us a reachable heroic example of a man with an education and an encounter. He was unbreakable.

For I will give you words and wisdom that none of your
adversaries will be able to resist or contradict.
Luke 21:15

> But if it is from God, you will not be able to stop these men;
> you will only find yourselves fighting against God.
> **Acts 5:39**

"We Stand UNDIVIDED" is a call to become irresistible and un-stoppable. The authority of the sent ones to prepare the way of the Lord. We cannot fret and we cannot fail. As the battle rages and the option of resigning from the front line is all too lucrative, remember His admonition and inspiration to the churches of Asia Minor that received letters from the Lord Jesus Christ at the hands of the Apostle John in Revelation chapters 2 and 3. Two themes that consistently surfaced within the majority of these churches: Christ hated (*his words*) when the Church approved, endorsed and accepted sexual immorality, including the teachings of the Nicolatians and the Spirit of Jezebel. But Christ rejoiced and promised significant blessings and rewards for those who remained faithful and overcame the persecution and tribulation which often plagued the Christian Church.

It is not time to rebrand the message. It is time to reclaim the message! UNDIVIDED, we can resist the spirit of deception which has persuaded a secular culture to deny God and remove moral restraints. UNDIVIDED, we can reverse this trend of biblical unbelief by making a bold presentation of truth. UNDIVIDED, the holy pulpits of Christ's Church can burn with passion, urgency and authority.

"Our times demand it. Our history compels it. Our future requires it. And God is watching," Rod Parsley, *Silent No More*.

As the world continues to become more confused morally, more corrupt politically, more chaotic militarily and on the brink of collapse financially — the Church must stand together as one body proclaiming the Kingdom of God. Simply, we are living in a post-Christian nation and we need each other. Jesus said, "A house divided cannot stand." In other words, we must stand UNDIVIDED!

Be of good cheer! These are the best of times! The worst of times will come. This is not *fatalism*. Contrarily, it is an anticipation that our new awareness will birth an awakening. This is *fineism!*

For the finest hour and the final hour of the Church has come! The pressure and the persecution will purge us of our apathy and apostasy, only to be replaced with a bold, strong, undivided Church reversing the trend of biblical unbelief.

For 2,000 years, the Church has been 'changing the world' because the Kingdom of God has come. I propose that the Church shifts gears and instead of 'changing the world,' let us prepare the world, for the King is coming!

For the finest hour and the final hour of the Church has come! The pressure and the persecution will purge us of our apathy and apostasy, only to be replaced with a bold, strong, undivided Church reversing the trend of biblical unbelief.

"Now, Lord, consider their threats and enable your servants to speak your word with great boldness. Stretch out your hand to heal and perform signs and wonders through the name of your holy servant Jesus."
After they prayed, the place where they were meeting was shaken. And they were all filled with the Holy Spirit and spoke the word of God boldly.
All the believers were one in heart and mind.
Acts 4:29-32

Final Word

Authentic Awakening

"The people of Israel, including the priests and the Levites,
have not kept themselves separate from the neighboring
peoples with their detestable practices, like those of the
Canaanites, Hittites, Perizzites, Jebusites, Ammonites,
Moabites, Egyptians and Amorites.
They have taken some of their daughters as wives for
themselves and their sons, and have mingled the holy race
with the peoples around them. And the leaders and officials
have led the way in this unfaithfulness."
Ezra 9:1-2

But you are a chosen people, a royal priesthood,
a holy nation, God's special possession,
that you may declare the praises of him who called you out of
darkness into his wonderful light.
1 Peter 2:9

An authentic awakening happens when the faith of the people becomes more than the religion of the few, but the identity of a holy nation. The biblical precedent is found in the great spiritual awakening that took place among the returning exiles through the leadership of Ezra and Nehemiah. Their forefathers were led into captivity because of their dual devotion to false idols and Elohim. This new generation was determined not to desecrate the temple. The book of Ezra never records false worship practices by returning Jewish exiles.

There was no mention of Baal, Ashtoreth, Molech, or high places. The temple was respected and carefully kept up.

Their worship was wonderful but their world view was wrong. They were intermingled with foreign spouses. Saving faith was present, but their cultural identity was absent. Social experts would have labeled them a pagan nation, more than a peculiar nation. Why? Because their worship was temple bound in the realm of private faith, which competed with and often lost against their public, mainstream, cultural assimilation. In other words, they easily switched between their church mode and their non-church mode ways of thinking and living.

Historians refer to the revival that occurred after the tribes gathered, through the ministry of Ezra and the supporting Levites, as a benchmark of true national renewal. The tangible result of the public square rally for the Book of the Law in Nehemiah chapter 7 was an unmistakable collective identity. They were not the Moabites. They were Israel. They were not the Amorites. They were Israel. Israel! Israel! Israel!

Christians are losing their lives in the East and losing their liberties in the West. Millions respond around the globe in solidarity when terrorists brutally murder French journalists in Paris. Where are the passionate protests against religious persecution when terrorists slay hundreds of Kenyan Christians or behead dozens of North African and Middle Eastern believers?

Collective identity mobilized the "I am Charlie Hebdo" protests. Sadly, our extent of concern is delegated to personal prayer for our poor brothers who are suffering martyrdom at the hands of madmen or lose their religious rights through defaming liberal lawsuits in America. Individual prayers are required as a minimum response. Where is the consistent, corporate and collective shared identity? Baptist, Pentecostal, Calvinist, Armenian, Protestant, Orthodox, Catholic, Evangelical, Traditional, Contemporary; the Church is not identical but we share the same identity — the Body of Christ. My blood is flowing in the Mediterranean Sea. My business closed down due to violent threats from intolerance. Jesus said, "This is my body." I am in Christ, so this is my body. If part of the Church suffers, than Christ is persecuted. If Christ is persecuted, than I am suffering.

The Church must organize and unify around our Core Beliefs and our Collective Identity to stand UNDIVIDED as a holy nation.

Is there a strategy to reverse Biblical unbelief, unite the Church and make ready the Lord's return? There is a Biblical order to gather the people of God before the heavens open. Prior to the four hundred years of silence leading up to the first coming of Jesus Christ, all the tribes gathered together under the leadership of Nehemiah for an authentic awakening. Israel was changed.

> The Church must organize and unify around our Core Beliefs and our Collective Identity to stand UNDIVIDED as a holy nation.

Prior to the coming of the Holy Spirit, all the God fearing men of the empire gathered in Jerusalem for the feast of Pentecost. The Church was changed. Prior to Christ's second coming, God will gather the remnant of Israel from the nations and the angels will gather the elect from the ends of the earth. The world will be changed.

Heaven comes to earth when the different tribes, as in Nehemiah's day, and the diverse tongues, as in the first Pentecost gather together. The proclamation of the Word through Ezra and the power of the Spirit through Peter caused the rebirth and birth of holy nations. God always raises up a voice and a visionary to pull together His people. That certain recognizable blast of the trumpet has sounded. Gather the congregations and denominations to stand UNDIVIDED! An awakening is at hand.

NOTES

PREFACE: CERTAIN SOUND

1. http://www.christianpost.com/news/why-atheism-will-replace-religion-author-economic-security-a-characteristic-of-godless-countries-100897/ Accessed Dec 20, 2014
2. George Barna, Seven Faith Tribes (Tyndale Momentum, 2009), 117
3. http://www.catholicleague.org/mikey-weinsteins-inflammatory-rhetoric/ Accessed March 25, 2014
4. "awareness." New Oxford American Dictionary. 2013
5. "awakening." New Oxford American Dictionary. 2013

INTRODUCTION: REVERSE THE TREND OF BIBLICAL UNBELIEF

1. John MacArthur, The Jesus You Can't Ignore (Thomas Nelson, 2008),19
2. Rod Parsley, The Cross (Charisma House, 2013), 127
3. Dan Cummins,http://www.charismanews.com/opinion/42246-2013-god-clergy-and-congress-poll-numbers-down-darwin-s-up-who-s-to-blame, Accessed December 12, 2013

CHAPTER 1: IT HAS BEGUN

1. https://www.barna.org/barna-update/article/21-transformation/252-barna-survey-examines-changes-in-worldview-among-christians-over-the-past-13-years#.UxoT0-dDLfA, Accessed March 6, 2009
2. George Barna, Seven Faith Tribes (Tyndale Momentum, 2009), 166
3. Indoctrination Documentary, 2011
4. http://www.relevantmagazine.com/slices/poll-religion-losing-its-influence#U00KAk5u3mhRerkt.99, Accessed May 31, 2013
5. http://usatoday30.usatoday.com/news/religion/2011-06-12-baptisms_11_ST_N.htm, Accessed June 6, 2012
6. http://www.bpnews.net/42559/pastors-task-force-releases-report-on-declining-baptisms, Accessed May 21,2014
7. http://www.pewforum.org/2012/10/09/nones-on-the-rise/, Accessed October 9, 2012

8. http://www.telegraph.co.uk/news/religion/8633540/Ageing-Church-of-England-will-be-dead-in-20-years.html, Accessed July 12, 2011

9. Dinesh D'Souza, What's so Great about Christianity (Regency Publishing, 2007), 5

10. http://www.charismanews.com/opinion/42246-2013-god-clergy-and-congress-poll-numbers-down-darwin-s-up-who-s-to-blame, Accessed 12/31/2013

11. "awakening." New Oxford American Dictionary. 2013

12. George Barna, Seven Faith Tribes (Tyndale Momentum, 2009), 149-150

13. https://www.barna.org/barna-update/culture/649-three-major-faith-and-culture-trends-for-2014#.Uz3cMa1DLfC, Accessed February 11, 2014

14. Rod Parsley, The Cross (Charisma House, 2013), 149

15. http://www.foxnews.com/opinion/2013/01/08/are-raising-generation-deluded-narcissists/, Accessed January 8, 2013

16. http://www.charismanews.com/opinion/42568-mr-obama-s-brand-of-christianity, Accessed January 8, 2014

17. Dinesh D'Souza, What's so Great about Christianity (Regency Publishing, 2007), 3

18. http://www.theatlantic.com/politics/archive/2014/02/the-changing-face-of-christian-politics/283859/, Accessed February 14, 2014

19. Robert Bork, Slouching Towards Gomorrah (Harper Collins, 1996), 62

CHAPTER 2: ABSENCE OF ACCOUNTABILITY

1. http://abcnews.go.com/blogs/politics/2014/04/bill-clinton-wouldnt-be-surprised-if-aliens-exist/, Accessed April 4, 2014

2. Charles Krauthammer, Things That Matter (Crown Forum, 2013),128

3. Dinesh D'Souza, What's so Great about Christianity (Regency Publishing, 2007), 24

4. Brannon Howse, One Nation Under Man (B&H Publishing Group, 2005), 124

5. Nancy Pearcey, Total Truth (Crossway Books, 2004), 167

6. Dinesh D'Souza, What's so Great about Christianity (Regency Publishing, 2007), 22

7. Michael Onfrey, Atheist Manifesto, (Arcade Publishing, 2007), 219

8. http://www.pewforum.org/2012/10/09/nones-on-the-rise/, Accessed October 9, 2012

9. Larry Taunton, Stand and Shine: Combatting Secularism in the Public Square www.FRC.org webcast, Accessed Oct 30, 2013
10. Dinesh D'Souza, What's so Great about Christianity (Regency Publishing, 2007), 23
11. Vox Dey, The Irrational Atheist (BenBella Books, 2008), 39
12. ibid
13. Rod Parsley, Living On Our Heads (Frontline Publishing, 2010), 157
14. http://sundayassembly.com/story/, Accessed April 5, 2014
15. http://www.salon.com/2013/09/22/atheism_starts_its_megachurch_is_it_a_religion_now/, Accessed September 22, 2013
16. https://holt.house.gov/press-releases/holt-proposes-darwin-day-to-recognize-205th-anniversary-of-charles-darwins-birth/, Accessed February 12, 2014
17. http://www.charismanews.com/us/42759-despite-nye-ham-debate-more-religious-people-still-celebrating-charles-darwin-s-birthday, Accessed February 12, 2014
18. Dinesh D'Souza, What's so Great about Christianity (Regency Publishing, 2007), 225
19. http://www.gallup.com/poll/21814/Evolution-Creationism-Intelligent-Design.aspx, Accessed April 16, 2014
20. Dinesh D'Souza, What's so Great about Christianity (Regency Publishing, 2007), 203
21. ibid, 28
22. ibid, 221
23. Charles Krauthammer, Things That Matter (Crown Forum, 2013), 3
24. ibid, 219
25. Dinesh D'Souza, What's so Great about Christianity (Regency Publishing, 2007), 214
26. Mark Tooley, http://www.faithstreet.com/onfaith/2013/10/21/christianity-is-not-going-away, Accessed March 20, 2014
27. http://www.faithstreet.com/onfaith/2013/10/21/christianity-is-not-going-away, Accessed April 17, 2014

CHAPTER 3: WRONG SIDE OF HISTORY

1. Rod Parsley, Culturally Incorrect (Thomas Nelson, 2007),126
2. http://www.colsoncenter.org/getstarted, Accessed April 17, 2014
3. American Heritage Dictionary

4. George Barna, Seven Faith Tribes (Tyndale Momentum, 2009), 166
5. Rod Parsley, Culturally Incorrect (Thomas Nelson, 2007), 86
6. Phillip Blom, A Wicked Company. The Forgotten Radicalism of the European Enlightenment (Basic Books, 2010), Intro
7. Rod Parsley, Culturally Incorrect (Thomas Nelson, 2007), 90
8. Larry Taunton, Stand and Shine: Combatting Secularism in the Public Square www.FRC.org webcast, Accessed Oct 30, 2013
9. Phillip Blom, A Wicked Company. The Forgotten Radicalism of the European Enlightenment (Basic Books, 2010), Intro
10. Vox Dey, The Irrational Atheist (BenBella Books, 2008), 37
11. French Revolution, Similarities to Modern America, Todd Friel on FRC Radio and online http://www.youtube.com/watch?v=1lovGSQ9miw#t=141, Accessed February 10, 2014
12. Indoctrination Documentary, 2011
13. ibid
14. N.T. Wright, Evil and the Justice and God (IVP Books, 2006) 21
15. ibid, 106
16. Charles Krauthammer, Things That Matter (Crown Forum, 2013), 8
17. George Barna, Seven Faith Tribes (Tyndale Momentum, 2009), 14
18. Vox Dey, The Irrational Atheist (BenBella Books, 2008), 68-77
19. Debbie Elliot, http://www.npr.org/templates/story/story.php?storyId=6439233, Accessed April 19, 2014
20. http://reason.com/assets/db/2014-millennials-report.pdf, pg 36, Accessed July 17, 2014
21. Nancy Pearcey, Total Truth (Crossway Books, 2004), 208

CHAPTER 4: CORE BELIEF #1, GOD IS THE CREATOR AND SOVEREIGN OVER HIS CREATION

1. https://www.youtube.com/watch?v=gHbYJfwFgOU Accessed April 22, 2014
2. http://www.foxnews.com/science/2014/04/24/8-biggest-mysteries-our-planet/?intcmp=features, Accessed April 25, 2014
3. Vox Dey, The Irrational Atheist (BenBella Books, 2008), 30
4. Dinesh D'Souza, What's so Great about Christianity (Regency Publishing, 2007), 116
5. ibid, 124
6. ibid, 124

7. http://www.answersingenesis.org/articles/au/days-of-decline-in-the-church?, Accessed Feb 10, 2014, December 13, 2013

8. Brannon Howse, One Nation Under Man (B&H Publishing Group, 2005), 137

9. ibid, 132

10. ibid, 125

11. http://www.worldviewchurch.org/wvc-digest/featured-articles/21243-take-it-from-the-darwinists-we-deliberately-ignore-the-evidence, Accessed February 13, 2014

12. Darrow Miller, ibid

13. Nancy Pearcey, Total Truth (Crossway Books, 2004), 183

14. ibid, 192

15. http://www.answersingenesis.org/articles/2013/09/13/abortionists-prayer, Accessed September 13, 2013

16. http://www.lifesitenews.com/news/jury-awards-couple-50-million-in-wrongful-birth-lawsuit, December 13, 2013

17. http://www.harpercollinsspeakersbureau.com/speaker/peter-singer/, Accessed April 23, 2014

18. http://www.oecdobserver.org/news/archivestory.php/aid/2480/Counting_the_hours.html, Accessed April 23, 2014

CHAPTER 5: CORE BELIEF #2, THE BIBLE IS 100% TRUE AND ITS MORAL TEACHINGS APPLY TODAY

1. http://online.wsj.com/news/articles/SB10001424127887324338604578326150289837608, Accessed April 23, 2014

2. Brannon Howse, One Nation Under Man (B&H Publishing Group, 2005), 199

3. http://www.cbn.com/spirituallife/biblestudyandtheology/jesus_prophecy_fulfilled.aspx, Accessed April 25, 2014

4. David Jeremiah, What In the World is Going On? (Thomas Nelson, 2010), 1

5. ibid, 2

6. Josh McDowell, Reasons Skeptics Should Consider Christianity, (Here's Life Publishers, 1981), 29

7. Focus on the Family, True U DVD series, Does God Exists?, 2012

8. ibid

9. Larry Taunton, Stand and Shine: Combatting Secularism in the Public Square www.FRC.org webcast, Accessed Oct 30, 2013

10. Nancy Pearcey, Total Truth (Crossway Books, 2004), 214
11. ibid, 157
12. http://en.wikipedia.org/wiki/Margaret_Sanger, Accessed April 25, 2014
13. Focus on the Family, True U. DVD series, Does God Exists?, 2012
14. New Oxford America Dictionary
15. Brannon Howse, One Nation Under Man (B&H Publishing Group, 2005), 152
16. ibid, 67

CHAPTER 6: CORE BELIEF #3, THE DEVIL IS REAL AND NOT MERELY A SYMBOLIC FIGURE

1. http://nymag.com/news/features/antonin-scalia-2013-10/index3.html, Accessed May 6, 2014
2. http://www.youtube.com/watch?v=ITLpTN-TiXQ, Accessed May 6, 2014
3. N.T. Wright, Evil and the Justice and God (IVP Books, 2006) 29
4. ibid, 111

CHAPTER 7: CORE BELIEF #4, MAN IS SINFUL AND SAVED BY GRACE

1. Rod Parsley, The Cross (Charisma House, 2013), 149
2. Dinesh D'Souza, What's so Great about Christianity (Regency Publishing, 2007), 287
3. Lady Gaga, Born this Way, Born this Way (Interscope Records, 2011), http://www.songlyrics.com/lady-gaga/born-this-way/
4. Macklemore and Ryan Lewis, Same Love, The Heist (Macklemore LLC, 2012),http://www.songlyrics.com/macklemore-ryan-lewis/same-love-lyrics/
5. Nancy Pearcey, Total Truth (Crossway Books, 2004), 211
6. ibid, 217
7. http://www.nj.com/politics/index.ssf/2015/05/nj_gay-to-straight_conversion_therapy_ban_left_int.html, Accessed June 2, 2015
8. http://en.wikipedia.org/wiki/The_New_England_Primer, Accessed May 14, 2014

CHAPTER 8: CORE BELIEF #5, JESUS IS THE SINLESS SAVIOR, THE SON OF GOD

1. Lee Strobel, The Case for the Real Jesus, (Zondervan, 2007)

2. http://www.huffingtonpost.com/2013/06/24/bono-jesus-focus-on-the-family_n_3491753.html, Accessed June 25, 2013
3. Lee Strobel, The Case for the Real Jesus, (Zondervan, 2007), 262
4. Michael Brown, The Real Kosher Jesus (Frontline, 2012), 99
5. Deepak Chopa, The Third Jesus, (Three Rivers Press, 2009)
6. Raza Aslan, The Zealot, the Life and Times of Jesus (Random House, 2013)
7. Ajith Fernando, The Supremacy of Christ, (Crossway Books, 1995), 51
8. ibid
9. ibid, 225
10. Rod Parsley, The Cross (Charisma House, 2013), 58
11. Dinesh D'Souza, What's so Great about Christianity (Regency Publishing, 2007), 297

CHAPTER 9: THE FOUNDATION TO THE CONSUMMATION

1. Michael Brown, The Real Kosher Jesus (Frontline, 2012), 133
2. ibid
3. ibid
4. Dinesh D'Souza, What's so Great about Christianity (Regency Publishing, 2007), 84
5. The New Matthew Henry Commentary (Zondervan, 2010)
6. Ann Carol, http://www.charismamag.com/spirit/church-ministry/19291-ag-and-cogic-leaders-unite-in-historic-pentecostal-meeting, Accessed December 4, 2013
7. http://www.charismamag.com/spirit/revival/20088-spirit-empowered-believers-praying-for-second-pentecostal-outpouring, Accessed April 1, 2014
8. http://www.christianpost.com/news/pope-francis-says-the-devil-is-keeping-evangelicals-and-catholics-divided-we-are-one-it-is-he-whos-persecuting-christians-today-139564/, Accessed June 2, 2015
9. http://www.charismanews.com/us/49661-southern-baptists-change-policy-on-speaking-in-tongues, Accessed June 2, 2015
10. http://www.christianpost.com/news/bishop-t-d-jakes-calls-on-the-church-to-end-racial-divide-and-fulfill-the-prayer-of-jesus-christ-that-we-may-be-one-video-139693/, Accessed June 2, 2015

CHAPTER 10: THE SPIRIT OF LAWLESSNESS

1. Todd Starnes, Godless America (Frontline, 2014), 8
2. ibid, 211
3. http://www.charismanews.com/us/41373-study-anti-christian-faith-sentiment-growing-at-breakneck-speed, Accessed October 15, 2013
4. ibid
5. ibid
6. ibid
7. http://blog.speakupmovement.org/church/religious-freedom/preparing-your-congregation-to-face-a-hostile-culture/, Accessed April 1, 2014
8. http://www.rzim.org/rzim-news/religious-freedom-in-the-workplace-statement-on-amicus-brief-filed-at-u-s-supreme-court/, Accessed January 30, 2014
9. http://www.charismanews.com/opinion/42740-are-true-christians-persecuted-in-america, Accessed February 11, 2014
10. http://www.pewforum.org/2014/01/14/religious-hostilities-reach-six-year-high/, Accessed May 24, 2014
11. http://www.washingtonpost.com/opinions/religious-liberty-is-americas-first-freedom/2014/03/21/498c0048-b128-11e3-a49e-76adc9210f19_story.html, Accessed March 21, 2014
12. http://www.charismanews.com/us/41443-the-tragic-inaction-of-the-church, Accessed October 21, 2013
13. http://en.wikipedia.org/wiki/Diocletianic_Persecution#Christians_in_the_army, Accessed May 24, 2014
14. http://drjamesdobson.org/about/commentaries/liberty-for-all, Accessed August 20, 2013
15. Todd Starnes, Godless America (Frontline, 2014), 63
16. http://www.gallup.com/poll/169640/sex-marriage-support-reaches-new-high.aspx, Accessed May 24, 2014
17. http://www.charismanews.com/us/40602-new-evangelicals-deny-anti-gay-rights-movement, Accessed August 13, 2013
18. http://cnsnews.com/news/article/obama-s-eeoc-nominee-society-should-not-tolerate-private-beliefs-adversely-affect, Accessed May 24, 2014
19. http://www.foxnews.com/opinion/2013/09/03/todd-american-dispatch-christian-bakery-closes-after-lgbt-threats-protests/, Accessed September 3, 2013
20. http://www.theblaze.com/stories/2013/08/23/court-says-christian-couples-refusal-to-photograph-same-sex-ceremony-was-illegal-why-you-will-be-made-to-care/, Accessed August 8, 2013

21. Todd Starnes, Godless America (Frontline, 2014), 63
22. ibid
23. ibid, 58
24. http://www.nytimes.com/2014/03/02/opinion/sunday/the-terms-of-our-surrender.html?_r=0, Accessed March 3, 2014

AUTHOR

S hawn Hyland is the founder of Move the Earth, a ministry which exists to reverse the trend of Biblical unbelief. Shawn is a graduate from World Harvest Bible College (Valor Christian College), Columbus, OH and ordained through the World Harvest Ministerial Alliance. He has appeared on FOX News, The Trinity Broadcasting Network and in national media publications as USA Today and Outreach Magazine. His teaching ministry spans a wide spectrum of local church congregations. He is married to Glennys Hyland. They reside with their four children on the Jersey Shore.

His current ministry campaign "We Stand — UNDIVIDED" has sparked an awakening of unity and urgency on the Jersey Shore with numerous pastors from across denominational backgrounds involved.